It's

Killing

Time in The Villages

Barbara —
Watch out!!

Tom Levine

fiction

ISBN 978-0-9729390-9-6

defiantworm@yahoo.com

printed in United States of America

for all the king's horses

By the same guy:

Bite Me!

Paradise Interrupted

The Last Opus of Hector Berlioz

Bass Fishing in Outer Space

The Light of a Day's Metallic

My Summer Vacation

It's

Killing

Time in The Villages

A little old woman is sitting on a park bench in The Villages. A man walks over and lowers himself to the far end of the bench. After a few moments, the woman looks over and asks, "Are you a stranger here?"

He replies, "I lived here years ago."

"Where were you since then?"

"In prison," he says.

"Oh my," she says. "Why did they put you there?"

He looks at her and very quietly says, "I killed my wife."

"Oh," says the woman. "So you're single..."

1

Time was North American whites toiled day after day in factories, on construction sites, in offices or hospitals, their annual reward a trip to Disneyworld with the family, the long term goal Heaven like the slaves who came before; but finding Heaven required forfeiting the mortal coil they cherished as they would an abusive parent. Now, twenty-first century, between Hell and Heaven lay a reward attainable by automobile. Nobody had to be good, observant or believe in Jesus to go there. They just had to live long enough and frugally, hope their health held out and believe in The Villages. If they scrimped and saved, maybe eschewed the Disney trips, redirected their tithe to a jar on the dresser, someday they might retire there. And become a Villageer.

At the zenith of the nation's STD rate, the fifties and up community would not disappoint. Vomited onto a fragile ecosystem already suffocating under concrete and northerners, this vast ecological disaster would ensure Republican dominance in Florida, enforcing the unimpeded plunder and ruin of the once paradisic peninsula while embracing Villageers with a kinder, gentler existence than ever they had known; a sandbox for the infirm, a panacea for the lonely and unappreciated, consolation for the incontinent and the bee's knees for the lazy. If distractions from thought, regrets, impotence and the purpose - emptied life are what modern man truly seeks, he will be satisfied here. If he treasures validation in membership, camaraderie and mild winters, he has arrived. With no prior chance to accumulate heroic sports reminiscences, the opportunity is now assured on one of the multitude of "safe" softball teams. Who loves nostalgia will find no further use of it, for the past idealized has returned to him missing only the loved ones who no longer populate it. Where Epcot never became the Experimental Community of Tomorrow, here is the Experimental Community of Yesterday. There is no racial segregation, no whites only signs, for in this universe only whites exist, like the tv they grew up watching. For a cheap thrill Villageers can view on tv in comfortable horror the depredations still faced by those remaining beyond their borders.

Retired insurance salesman Joe Beasley had stepped from Iowa into a dream he'd never had the prescience to invent while sleeping; stalked by women he had slavered after from the sexual crucible of adolescence to the desperation of adulthood with fantasy his only hope. By only remaining motionless while chemistry advanced, he had inherited his place in a flesh-potbelly paradise, the orbits of celestial bodies having decayed into his. Joe Beasley, fornicator of cheerleaders, executives, radio personalities, Weeki Wachee mermaids; his for the taking – perhaps overripe but appreciative and generous. Whoda thunk it? For him life did began after forty; well after.

Calloused, pink hand around a chilled mug of Coca Cola, Joe sat at the bar in Bud Tinsley's house, feeling like a man who might someday need new worlds to conquer. One of his posse, Bud Tinsley was lounging a couple stools over.

"Hey I just remembered," Bud said, "I'm peeing by the oak tree night before last and this hot broad comes around the corner and catches me. I'm trying to put it away and you know what she says?"

"Nope."

"She says, 'I like a man who pees in his yard.' And she just keeps walking. By the time I thought of something to say, she's gone."

"Well Bud, sounds like a woman with standards a man can appreciate."

"I hope I see her again."

"Just keep peein' in the yard. She'll be back. Men like that are hard to find." Beasley glanced at his watch. "Say Bud," he said casually, "I just remembered - I left Candy Barrington out there on the lawn. You might want to check if she's still there."

"Really?" Bud said, shooting upright. "Candy? The Congresswoman?"

"Yup. Maybe you could appropriate somethin'."

"Shit. A Congresswoman." Bud filled with images of Roman columns and domes. "Is she awake?"

"Out like a wet cigaret. Probably still time for you to

9

pop your little blue pill."

Bud pulled back the picture window curtain and stole a quick look, then put hand quickly to mouth. "You tell anybody else?"

Joe shook his head like a tranquilized rhinoceros. "If you're that worried about it, drag her in here."

"Yeah. No. I like it better outside. Cleaner, you know."

Joe nodded with the air of a man who'd been there – done that. "But hey – you know, if she has good dreams, she might come around looking for you next time." He laughed heartily.

"No, Joe, she'll probably just dream of you, the Viagra- free King of Testosteronia."

"Yep. That is a kind of ace in the hole, ... if you know what I mean."

"Yeah. I know what you mean," Bud said, standing and stretching his arms. "Hey look. I'm a little restless. Think I'll just take a little walk outside, check out the night air."

"Sure. If you see some o' that night air in the lawn, I recommend you roll her onto her belly if she ain't already. That's her best side."

"Thanks, Joe. Just going for a stroll."

Joe raised a hand in "so long" and waited for Bud's front door to shut before he stopped holding in a joyous chuckle. He walked to the window and slightly put his face beyond the curtain, saw Bud stop before a heap on the lawn, say something to it, then prod it with a foot. Soon

Bud stood in a puddle of pants. To be inconspicuous, he knelt in the damp grass and gingerly started to raise the hem of a skirt which, like a weird remote control, coincided with the blaze of floodlights and flashbulbs.

Barney Jenkins twisted and looked up from the grass at the turgid Villageer. "Hey Bud," he chortled, "I never knew you cared!"

Bud just said, "Ah shit." His mental crash could not translate to his extension, whose pride was irrepressible. To preserve some modicum of dignity, Tinsley stood, stepped out of his pants-puddle and returned to his house, shooting a moon from the doorway.

As they passed, Bud flashed Beasley a recognition of infinite betrayal. Joe just said, "Gotcha, Bud," and headed for his golf cart. Well, he thought, triumphantly finishing off his Coca Cola, there's the homeowners association off our backs for awhile.

Jenkins intercepted him with a clap on the back. "Well done, Joe. How'd you know the jerk would go for that?"

"Don't sell yourself short, Barn. You looked pretty sweet out there. Kinda like candy."

After high-fiving all around, Joe Beasley leaned back in his cart and visualized cable tv coming into his house. Then he tried to recall every woman he'd penetrated since buying into The Villages lifestyle. Let's go with categories, he thought. Short, tall, state of origin…no, that's boring. A man could go that route anywhere. How about "occupations." He most relished women of authority: cops had been a generous category, plenty of banter about parking violations, you gonna put me under abreast, that sort of things. He did a few retired teachers, that was good, always puns to be made depending on their specialty. Almost got a high school principal. "That would have been something," he lamented, "having sex with the principal. Then you know you're bullet proof. Well, a man has to have goals, the unseen land, frontiers. There was the head of The Villages Wastewater Department. Not too shabby."

His thoughts drifted back to the first billboard he saw promoting The Villages lifestyle, showing a man about his age following through life on his golf swing. He was on a road trip and it flitted by beside U.S.441 just south of Leesburg.

"That isn't the kind of swinging they were talking about." He chuckled, eternally grateful to have met Phil Swanson who clued him into the party going on out there, chilled by the thought that without that chance meeting, he probably never would be where he is today and his entire life, instead of just the first two-thirds of it, would have been for nothing.

Spring break every day, he thought.

2

M any residents of The Villages were surprised yet again by the dawning of another day upon them. What to do, what to do with this bonus. As sun burned through fog, you thought you could squint and make out std's wafting along on the early breeze, feel them, almost hear them singing along with Mitch.

Each fist around a 10 ounce dumbbell, Margaret Truman's pink leotard careened around the corner barely able to keep up with her startling pink legs. Fartamongus P. Farquard III waved to her from his Thunderbird golfcart, bounced off the road and front-ended a smiling fire hydrant. Margaret kept churning like an escaped egg beater down the sidewalk. Less energetic Villageers, beyond the clutches of sensuality and exercise, eternity clawing at them since they awoke that morning, marveled at her energy from benches and reminisced the golf swing they never had.

Margaret had escaped again, outpaced their fate, stuck to the road to elsewhere, imbued with the juices of The

Villages, inoculated against decay by the many activities. She noticed an oddly personal sized lump in a nearby ditch. With naught else impinging upon her time, she investigated.

Attendees at Joe Beasley's wake mostly were female, middle-age, roundish butted and variously-bosomed. They felt like every child whose coveted helium balloon had burst with its string still clutched in her tiny fist. Where would ever they find another one like that in The Villages? Would they be forced to roam beyond their blissful isolation? The implications of the predicament were striking them like centenarian Emily Barnhorst's bowling ball painstakingly wending its way through the pins until all have fallen. Ocala? God forbid. Please. Leesburg?!? Might as well return to Ohio. Bignocular-equipped males attended distantly from a sense of personal obligation to survey this field of uprooted petunias before they might wilt, capitalize on an emotional moment or take note for the future. Jim Baxter's eyes protruded beyond his stamen when he realized they all were gold slippered, every last one of them. Then they fell back from the exertion.

So much for a period of mourning, Jim thought, shaking his head in wonder. Somebody should have knocked Joe off a long time ago.

God's emissary from The Church of the '57 Chevy Convertible, the right Reverend Amos Gilhooly positioned the Holy Stepladder in the parking lot, ascended to the top, then hopped onto the red hood of the sacred vehicle, backed up by shimmering laurel oaks. He brought Eulogy 9b, b for Beasley as it were, b for Bettendorf, whence he

14

emerged and b for the Boss. "Dying is not something you do," the Methodist preacher began, "it's everything you won't do. In the case of the magnificent Joe Beasley, it's every*body* he won't do. If you're a woman who never knew the charms of The Great Depantsinator, you simply missed your chance; perhaps you should have butted in line. All others, you multitudes, be glad for what you had, for, unlike Jesus, it will come not again; in any shape or form, for a man of Beasley's abilities, verve and willingness does not rise up every day like the common cold or hemorrhoids."

Gilhooly could not have imagined how far from the mark this last sentence almost was. He continued, "No, he rose every day like the sun, washing the landscape in warmth and light. Men too should mourn the passing of Joe Beasley for he gave us an ideal to strive for, a local hero to worship, and like the sun, we found comfort in knowing he also rises.

"For many of us life is a paradox – sad because we are happy, long because we are short and hard because we are soft. But we had Joe to ease our burden, lifting it from our bent shoulders and placing it on his own resilient ones. No one knew how he came to be this way, as they say, God's gift to women - of The Villages. But this was his true calling, this the population he faithfully served. Elsewhere Joe would have been just a regular Joe Shmo but he was equal to his time and place and opportunity. He made perfect the greatest place to live. He made The Villages the greatest place for a middle-aged woman to live. And in this he did his part to make America great again. He did not come with your real estate contract or your home owner's association. He simply came here with the best of motivations and in so doing, kept the promise of that document of documents, the United States Declaration of Independence.

Hand over heart Gilhooly commanded all to join in the Pledge of Allegiance, which they fervently did. He then commanded they recite it backwards. A few tried but this was generally met with objections. It had the desired effect of calming everyone back down. The reverend dropped the idea like it was a rattlesnake and resumed. "Joe Beasley was an egalitarian man, one who had much to offer and was not stingy with it," the pastor boomed, "a tender patriot on the battlefield of love, he believed women also are created equal and entitled not only to the pursuit but the capture of that elusive quality we call happiness. So he ran slowly, a hard man not to catch.

"Yes, he sure was," Lizzie Turnbull was heard muttering between sobs, her head slowly shifting side to side like a bobble-head cooter's.

"Much like Tinker Bell, Joe flitted one flower to the next, showering them in Pixie dust on his way."

This allusion to the much beloved fairy fomented a female chorus of groans and sobs accompanied by snickers and eye rolling from a few men.

"And the women of The Villages were God's gift to Joe. Now that Joe is with his Maker, let us pray that God is merciful and understanding of the drives with which He imbued us all and that He lets the gift keep on giving. With all that Joe Beasley will not do on Earth, we must do it in his name. Many speak of their bucket list. Joe Beasley never did for it is more of death than life. When someone says "it's on my bucket list," that is his excuse for never doing it. A bucket list is just a mythical place where good intentions go to die. Live, like Joe Beasley did, live now, like it's all you've got, not in the very unreliable future. Let this be his legacy. By keeping alive the spirit of Joe, we keep him here with us. Remember – no one ever kissed... a bucket list."

Sugar plum fairies dancing in all the men's heads, the Most Reverend Gilhooly finished with a reminder always to say, "We believe in Tinker Bell and Joe Beasley that neither will ever truly die. Now repeat after me...."

"Tinker Bell has a lots better body than Joe," John Smith mumbled to general agreement in his vicinity as the phrase was chanted.

"I always wished they didn't put that dress on her," Niles Standish added to enthusiastically grim nods as the crowd began dispersing.

"Well, you know those fairies in Fantasia are nekkid," Jim Baxter pointed out, punching Smith in the shoulder.

"I never noticed that," Standish regretted, rubbing his chin thoughtfully.

"You probably never saw Fantasia."

No dearth of moist eye led the fallen from the stricken area, looking to, not at each other, with not jealously but deep understanding and empathy. Never competitors for Beasley's favors, they had felt more like a sports team battling the clock. Well into the third quarter, God had

17

taken their balls and gone home.

Working up the obit, Cub reporter from the Villages Sun, Jimmy Oldson drove to The Next Phase. He read aloud the gravestone, "Here Lies Joe Beasley. May he rest in peace of ass." Jimmy couldn't help filling with awe for any man with such a send-off. As he pondered how to work it into his assignment, he sensed Maxine Falderall standing beside him, dressed in pitch black.

"Did you know Mr. Beasley?" he asked, hoping for some human interest.

"I knew him a long, long time ago," she answered quietly. "When he was so shy and so used to girls who couldn't see the fine boy inside that he couldn't believe I wanted him." She gazed tragically at the reporter. "He didn't have to stay a virgin for so long...and neither did I."

Here could be the Obit of the Week, Oldson thought, picturing the Sun's most coveted award adorning his dresser. He offered her his arm. "Would you like to have lunch?"

She looked up at his orange hair and brown eyes and smiled, saying, "Very much, young man. Give me just a minute and I'll meet you at your car."

They settled in at The Last Supper drive-in with Barrabas burgers all the way and chocolate shakes. "Joe was such a respectful young man," she said. "He never ogled girls or whistled or anything; always polite. Sometimes he'd even carry my books to school. One day some young hoodlums teased me because of my braces and he put up his dukes. He told them what to expect if they bothered me again."

"Mr. Beasley was something of a bad-ass then."

"Oh no," she said, scandalized by the idea. "He just knew what was right and wrong...a distinction that doesn't seem too clear around here."

"What do you mean by that?" Oldson probed.

Falderall continued, "Nobody else ever was willing to fight for me. I suppose I got too focused on Joe. It just never happened. He started to get pimples and lost what self confidence he might have had. It never happened for us."

"What never happened?"

"Well, sex of course. It just never happened."

"I suppose you went your separate ways and found love elsewhere," the reporter filled in.

Maxine gazed at him with consternation. "Oh no. I mean it never happened at all. Then I followed Joe here and still it didn't happen, small consolation that it would have been. I was too old, I suppose."

Oldson sat back absorbing the import of what he had heard and carefully formulating his follow up. He leaned across the table. "Are you telling me you're a virgin?"

Falderall's eyes dropped as she nodded coquettishly.

"Waiting for Mr. Beasley?" he asked, awash in wonder while visualizing the by-line.

"He was worth it... or would have been anyway. I guess."

"And now he's dead," Jimmy Oldson said with moist eyes, a genesis of passion for this comely senior citizen

19

welling up inside him greater than any he had felt for a woman. He urgently wanted to hug her. And more. Much more.

"Now that he's gone, what will you do?"

"I don't know," she said, looking up into the freckled picture of Norman Rockwell's America. "I just don't know."

3

P eople frequently find the end of their tether in The Villages but there's no predicting exactly where in the community it will draw tight. It may be outside as easily as in. Sheer familiarity has robbed dying of whatever luster it may possess in communities of lower frequency. Sometimes, especially if a Villageer happens to tip over in the backyard, the physically fit spouse may just dig a hole right there and be done with it. So the law prohibiting backyard burial is vigorously enforced, residents encouraged to report anything suspicious.

Murder among the many actions discouraged there, though not so stridently opposed as cable tv, Beasley's relocation to the more austere afterlife engineered by a mere mortal never was seriously considered by local officials. However it was a possibility reporter Oldson had ruminated on extensively.

"After all," he was told by the mayor's secretary, "enforcing the city code consumes time and manpower enough without sweating trivialities. The dead are no longer participating and there are more on the way."

"That seems a little callous," Oldson responded.

"Far from it," she said. "In fact we're planning a new village called Deadwood. There residents or their relatives can purchase a house and populate it with wax figures of their loved ones who have passed beyond The Villages. 'Arrangers' will go in periodically and adjust their positions, their clothes, alter facial expressions, switch the tv channel between their favorite shows, change out the wax fruit on the dining room table, set out different tv dinners, mess up the towels in the bathroom, diminish the toilet paper roll, that sort of thing. Registered family over fifty will be given keys and allowed to visit at any time for up to a week."

"Hmmm. Can they take them to church on Sunday?" Jimmy asked brightly.

"The local clergy will make house calls. So as you can see, we are anything but callous."

"Wow!" Oldson concluded, "You sure aren't. That's the nicest thing I ever heard of."

"You could do a story about it."

"I sure could!"

Softball is huge in the Villages, part of the overall plan to keep residents moving until they get back in bed at night, with fun slogans like FOUL BALLS not FOUL PLAY and KILL the UMP. He's Expendable.

John Smith was on 12 of the 250 The Villages softball teams, divided equally among the sectors of Lake Humpter, Spanish Bedsprings and Blownwood. A few times a month he actually played against himself, accomplished by trading a toupee for a hat and glasses every half inning. Strictly against the omnipotent Villages softball rules, this was punishable by banishment from the league. Smith assessed his playing days probably numbered anyway, his wearing of a colostomy bag on the field a major violation; manager, batman and base coach jobs reserved for such as him. It was only a matter of time before the puffy shirt failed – a collision at first base, a hard tag, a simple untimely malfunction. He, like his waste, would be ejected. Once out he's out for good so he was getting in as much playing as possible. At least they've got me in the outfield, he assured himself.

You never know, he thought, being a "bag half empty" optimist, I could go on for a long time this way. Only one Villageer knew about it and he's not going to tell.

Smith recalled the night he and Joe Beasley had succeeded simultaneously with one liberal minded woman they had met at The End Zone sports bar. By Beasley's insistence on going first, he was sure Joe had noticed though it never was mentioned.

Anyway, he mused, I'm sure not the only one. Frank with his fake doctor's report exonerating him of any association with diabetes. Ron with his pacemaker, George with his phony birth certificate, he's 95 if he's a day; kept him from getting stuck in the soft bat league. And Sid who's not even a man. Most everybody's hiding something.

Pocahontas Smith was painting Daisies on his fresh colostomy bag as her husband wolfed down lunch, running late for the game, as was his custom, hoping to fill the bag and refresh it before leaving the house. The new food had the desired effect and John headed to the ballpark fresh as a flower.

The team, wearing shirts proclaiming Old Farts are Stronger, already was wandering around on the field when he arrived and saw the roster tacked to the dugout wall with J. Smith on the dreaded second base. The hormones of trepidation shot through like a lightning bolt, pushing lunch through him and out.

"Get out there, Smith," the coach growled as the bag was filling. "The game's starting."

When she saw her man listlessly parking his golfcart on the front lawn, Pocahontas Smith knew something was terribly wrong. She performed a naked fartwheeel in front of their townhouse in hopes of showing him that all was not lost. He simply stared with suppressed envy as he trudged by her toward the security of home.

John slumped onto the red velvet couch, looking straight ahead as if he had glimpsed infinity and it was on the wall. "Well, I had a full bag but things were okay," he began. "I just get through the first inning and go change it out. Two out, man on first, here comes Bob Barker barreling in on a fielder's choice. I take the toss from third and he slides feet first, grabs me to try and not overshoot the base." Jim shook his head ruefully. "Shit flyin' everywhere."

Pocahontas frowned sympathetically.

"The ump walks over holding his nose, gives me the thumb and says, 'Looks like your luck's run out.' A real comedian.

"Then Bob Barker calls me a sonofabitch and takes a swing at me."

"If only the fielder had chosen first," Jim's wife cooed tragically, rubbing his nape.

"Yeah. If only. Life's full of those. If only cactuses didn't have thorns. If only the sky had naked women painted on it like the Pristine Chapel over in Europe. If only I didn't crap out my side. You can't think that way. It'll drive you nuts."

Pocahontas Smith nodded thoughtful appreciation of these truths while silently vowing to compensate for the natural if only's of life.

4

Finally someone had lost his virginity with Maxine Falderall while she lost hers and definitely couldn't find it anywhere. A watershed moment for the lovers, she and Jimmy Oldson were ready and willing to move on after a little more practice. Soon an event of staggering proportions would overshadow the obit of Joe Beasley and rock the very foundations of The Villages. The freckled reporter was exquisitely positioned to take Story of the Year.

Jimmy was composing a letter to his mother in Orla Vista and wondering what she'd think about him having a girlfriend fifteen years her senior. Maxine was in the bathroom examining a suspicious rounding in her front. She had tried to exorcise the bulge with exercise but it grew ever more prominent. In the face of the exercise offensive, her friends in the Reborn Women's Club worried that a tumor was growing or worse, she had been inseminated by Aliens. Or O'bama.

Three days later Jimmy Oldson kept an appointment

with the crusty editor of the Village Sun, Verry White. Oldson stood expectantly before the desk. "If what you say is true, this story is bigger than the Villages." White chomped on his Dutch Master, then leaned over his desk. "Those folks down in Lantana will pay a hundred grand for this."

"Well, sir, I was there. Got it straight from the doctor, who seemed like he was gonna go crazy or something. 'How old did you say you are?' he yells at Maxine. 'Fifty-six,' she says all sweet like she always is."

"'I want to see your birth certificate,' he's almost roaring at her now."

"'Why?'" she says.

"'Because,' he says, leaning down to her face, 'I don't believe you.'"

"'I don't have my birth certificate with me,' she says."

"'Do you have your driver license?'"

"'Well,' she says, 'I don't know...'"

"'Go ahead, Maxine,' I tell her, 'show him your license.'"

"She digs into her purse and comes up with it. 'Here's my driver's license,' she says. And she hands it to him just as pretty as you please.

"The doctor takes one look at it and yells, 'So you *were* lying. You're actually sixty."

I thought the guy was going to jump out the window."

"You'd think he'd be excited," White put in.

"He was excited alright. But it's like it makes him so mad."

27

"Turned his world upside down. Some people don't like that."

"The thing is," Oldson added with an air of confidentiality, "there's been older ones."

"I didn't know that," said White, crestfallen. "Maybe they'll go ten thousand."

"Here's the kicker," Oldson said. "All the older ones were invitro fertilization, borrowed eggs, petri dishes, all that. Maxine is the oldest natural one. Ever"

"And how do we know this?" White said, glancing sideways at his cub reporter.

"What you're thinking right now," he said, "that's how."

The Dutch Master plummeted to the floor.

"It gets better." Oldson said, leaning over and retrieving his boss's cigar and then, to White's ever-growing astonishment, putting it between his own teeth and having a puff before handing it back while hacking his brains out. "It was her first time," he squeaked out.

"That's no big deal."

"To have sex."

"That's preposterous."

"Mine too."

When the cigar fell from White's jaws this time it crashed to the floor like a truckload of frozen turkeys. Inside his skull a carousel of headlines displaced Verry White's brain. As *Harold and Maude: the Reproduction* passed by, he fainted.

Oldson blew some second hand cigar smoke into the

28

editor's face who came around raving. "Love Story meets the Ten Commandments? I don't know where to go with this. Should we jump right to the movie? The documentary?"

Oldson hands him the phone. "Just call the Enquirer. They'll know what to do."

5

"I sure never saw that coming," Jimmy the Geek said, joylessly stirring a martini olive with his finger. "Thousand to one odds on Joe Beasley and one taker. I wonder if old Maxine had some inside info."

"Inside info? Like what? A pipeline to the Grim Reaper?" Barry the Croation said, sprawling on the stained couch with his bowl of regular Cheerios in orange juice.

"I think it might have taken Death by surprise. Joe was healthy as a horse. A stallion in fact. What got him anyway?"

"I never heard. Natural is all they said."

"You musta heard somethin' out there. Even I heard a lotta people are lookin' at Bud Tinsley."

"Tinsley, eh? Let me check the line on him....no, nothing unusual. It's pretty quiet out there."

"You could hear a pin drop."

"On a sofa. Say, why the Hell did you put orange juice on your cereal?"

"Tastes great. Used to throw Cheerios into my juice when Mama wasn't looking. Vowed when I could do what I wanted, I'd just pour it all over 'em. You should try it."

"They oughta lock you up, you know that don't you?"

Barry just smiled. "You ever do it, you'll kick yourself for all those wasted years. Slice of banana in there, it's what Cheerios were made for."

"I don't eat 'em anyway, even the sane way. They look stupid."

"What'd she bet?"

The Geek smiled. "A dollar."

"That's lucky. She could have put you out of business with that line."

"You better believe it." They both laughed and the Geek shook his head. "Smells fishy, Barry, but I can't figure out what kind of fish."

"When did the old cutey lay it down?"

"Six months ago. Told me to just keep rolling it over. It was a great stretch. Rolled it over a hundred and seventy times."

"Thought that was your IRA huh?"

"Then I rolled snake eyes."

"What are the odds on me today?"

"Well Barry, let's just have a look at the board. You know you can't bet on yourself."

"Yeah sure. That'd be a bad bet anyway. Look at me."

"I'm lookin' at you Barry but I ain't convinced. Let's look at the spread. Here you are. Jesus! Sixty to one. You just go to the doctor? Somebody got a hit out on you?"

"Lemme see that. Twelve hundred to one. That's more like it. Bullet proof. Better than Beasley."

"That's cause Joe was having sex."

"You think I'm not?"

"Maybe my sources are unreliable and you have unduly inflated odds. Word gets out they'll go down. There's a murderer out there you know.

"Just keep it to yourself."

"Sure. Had you goin' for a second though."

"Anything down on me?"

"No takers. Today. That's some long odds. You gotta have a crystal ball for that."

"You'll let me know, right?"

"Can't do it, Barry. All I got's my reputation. I'm startin' a lottery. Why don't you try that?"

"What's the catch?"

"No catch. You just name a day when nobody in The Villages kicks the bucket. Pays five hundred to one. That's some generous odds."

"Hmm. That include day trippers?"

"Hadn't thought of that. I'll say no. You wanta call a nonresident dyin', give you two-fifty"

"What?!? Too low."

"And I thought you were a gambling man."

6

Barney Jenkins' time had come. Not only was he watching cable tv, illicitly installed in the code enforcement vacuum left by the compromise of Bud Tinsley, but gold slippers were glittering everywhere he looked and he was removing them. His dance card was full and he was getting full. Sorry Joe, he thought, we never appreciated the burden you carried for us. Jenkins was starting to slip, forgetting who he was with and guessing wrong half the time. Pretty soon they all started actually looking the same. Monday night he had arranged to meet Betty Blooper at the Rialto, forgot and then invited The Villages prostitute Budget Bardoe. They both showed up and nobody was willing to budge so they just wound up in a Villages sandwich.

"That's it," Barney mused, "I'm taking a month off and going fishing and things like that. Maybe take up roller skating. Never thought I'd see the day."

That afternoon found Barney casting rubber worm into the mysterious depths of Lake Humpter. This lured women more than bass and he felt the dissatisfaction of the jaded, no longer desiring what once gave life meaning. Two-thirds of the men walking by informed Barney that fishing from the boardwalk was not allowed. "Can't even go fishing," he fumed. "Might as well kill myself. Or come up with something else to stay on the green side for."

Riding high on his recent Gonzo journalistic coup and working on a hunch, Jimmy Oldson approached the discommoded sportsman, National Enquirer in hand.

"Excuse me," he said, "I'm Jimmy Oldson."

"Screw you, punk. You don't even live here. Waddayou care if I'm fishing anyway. Am I hurting somebody? You an animal rights nutjob? I ain't even hurtin' any fish. Not that I don't want to."

Surprised by this reception, the sweet boy felt he may finally have contacted the crusty underworld of The Villages. He persevered.

"I'm a reporter for the Village Sun. Just wondering what you might think about this story."

"Well I'm the Village Sunofabitch. And I think who gives a crap about an old lady getting pregnant? It's disgusting if anything."

"Hey. Watch it."

"You wanted my opinion, you got it. Most people don't want my opinion. I don't even want my opinion. The thing'll probably be born old, look like Jimmy Durante or John McCain."

Oldson regained his professional objectivity despite the horrifying images. He cleared his throat. "You know her?"

"Not really. I know of her, keyword 'of.' Whadda you care? I'm not Satan."

"I never indicated you were."

"You're the reporter. Who the Hell else you think could make that happen?"

"Just following up," the reporter hissed.

"Well follow up somewhere else. I'm trying to fish."

"Caught anything?"

"Now that would be a story."

"Did you know Joe Beasley?"

"Of course I knew Joe. Hey, what is this anyway?" Barney leaned his rod against a fake piling. "Joe was a friend of mine."

"Do you know how he died?"

"Yeah. He stopped farting." He looked Oldson in the eye. "That'll work for anybody."

"But you don't know why he stopped."

"I ain't the coroner. I figured Susie finally got him."

Now we're getting somewhere, the keen reporter thought. "Who's Susie?"

"Susie Syphilis."

"Oh. Yeah, sure. Why her?"

"Why not?"

"Coulda been Gonorreah Gloria," Oldson muttered.

"What's that?"

"Nothing."

An elderly gentleman walked up. "I see the fishing rod," he said. "I just thought you should know, young man, before you get in trouble, there's no fishing here."

"%!&* you, Hitler. What makes you think it's his rod? You can't see me standing here? What am I, chopped liver?" Jenkins grabbed the rod and cast, getting a loose-loop snarl. "This is the highlight of my day so far. Why don't you make it even brighter and die? Over there. This reporter here is very interested in stuff like that. That's his beat. The dead beat."

The man hurried off, saying, "No need to be rude."

"Go to Hell, faggot," Barney further directed. "Oh, Sorry."

"Are you always like this?" Oldson continued.

"You mean this charming?"

"Yes."

"Look at me. I'm old. I've fornicated every unmarried woman in The Villages. Thought I'd go fishing and maybe relive my youth or something and all I get is this (displaying the snarl). How would you be?"

"Every woman?"

"Hey look. That's not for publication. You pissed me off into saying that."

"Don't worry. I don't even know your name. How about Maxine?"

"How about Maxine what? Oh, you mean Rosemary. What are you up to? I told you I'm not the father."

"How do you know? You said you had sex with her."

"Watch your mouth Carrot Top."

"Sorry. One more thing. Do you think foul play may have been involved in the demise of Mr. Beasley?"

"What?!? Foul balls more likely. And for the record he didn't get no demise. He got death. That's what Joe's got right now. It's real quiet and I doubt he likes it much but it's startin' to look pretty good to me."

Jenkins reeled the snarled line onto the spool. "Now if you don't mind, I think I'll go home and try to take a shit. That should eat up some time."

Oldson offered his card. Jenkins took it, flossed briefly and handed it back. "Thanks," he said and headed down the boardwalk to his &%#!ing golfcart.

Oldson remained behind awhile, imagining the accolades over his cracking of The Villages' most infamous murder. Natural death, he thought. Not likely. Anyway, nothing more natural than murder. So many suspects, so few bodies. Beasley was a walking death certificate. Every hopeful Villagara enabled man made redundant by Boner Beasley; a jealous husband, all the women Beasley two or three-timed. Even dear Maxine vengeful after a squandered life. This crabby guy fishing... must find out who he is. I think he knows stuff.

Maxine Falderall was hiding from the paparazzi in Jimmy Oldson's Lady Lake apartment. She found herself remarkably liberated by the exit of Beasley, like she'd been tied by the neck to a post and now she could look in all directions. She looked forward to Oldson's arrival home to hear about his day and the affairs of the world.

Jimmy poked his head in the door. "Where's my little

celeb?"

He looked behind the couch. "Not here," he said. He checked the broom closet. "Or here..."

Maxine was trying hard to stifle giggles as he walked right past the bathtub where she was standing behind the shower curtain. "Not here," Oldson said, apparently puzzled. "Where in the world can she be?"

As he exited the room, he heard, "Here I am!" as Maxine flung open the curtain.

She was showing more and the reporter filled with wonder at the idea of the tiny life he had started in there, a nursery in readiness for the last forty-some years with nothing to nurture. This was a womb with tenacity. He wondered how many wombs never used there must be in the world and how that must feel for the women carrying them around like an umbrella on a sunny day. He, Jimmy Oldson, born halfway through the crucible, had emerged and granted this one, in the nick of time, its purpose.

Maxine had a youthful blush to her cheeks and actually seemed to be growing younger as her fetus aged. Jimmy Oldson thought he might be falling in love.

He gallantly helped her out the tub and they held hands on the couch.

"And what did the cub reporter for a great metropolitan newspaper do today?" she asked with enthusiasm.

"Oh, I was just going around talking to people." He looked his lover in the eyes. "Maxy, do you think Joe Beasley might have been killed?"

Her hand let go his and went to her mouth. "No. Oh

God no. This is The Villages."

Oldson only said Umm and nodded his head.

"Do you think he was killed?" she said, searching his face for the answer. "Who would do such a thing to my lovely boy?"

Oldson was startled. "I thought I was your lovely boy."

After a pause Maxine said. "You did what Joe never did, didn't you? You are my man."

For the first time, Jimmy Oldson felt like a man, a real fight and die for his woman man. He regretted bringing Maxine pain. "I'm sorry. It just seemed odd where his body was found. I'm told he wasn't a jogger or a walker, no golfcart around. My nose for news makes me wonder what he was doing out there."

"You're right. Maybe he wasn't doing anything there. Maybe he was left there."

Oldson nodded. "And no details in the coroner's report. Died of natural causes. What does that mean?"

"A tree fell on you." She reclaimed his hand and placed it on her belly. "Let's think about the future, not the past."

"I can't feel anything."

"Well, not yet silly. It's very small."

"I wonder if it's a boy."

"I think it is," Maxine cooed.

"Should we find out?"

"No. That's not nature's way. I want you to be

surprised."

"Maxine, I...I think I love you."

"I know."

Reporters were crawling all over The Villages trying to find a fresh angle on the big story. And trying to smoke out Maxine Falderall. This was an unexpected windfall for the local women, to whom the newsmen were what's known as "fresh meat." Below The Villages average in age and interested in conversation, The Reborn Women's Club held a meeting.

Margaret Truman took the podium. "Look. This isn't going to last forever. Pretty soon a wooden puppet is going to come to life somewhere and Falderall will be yesterday's vagina. I say now is the time to strike."

Budget Bardoe stood looking at the floor, confident she knew where the speaker was heading with this. Slowly she raised her head, the pearliest of whites were revealed and she said almost imperceptibly, "Orgy." Next to her Dinah Snore mumbled it on down the line. Betty Blooper endowed it with a few more decibels. The chant went up from the membership.

"We've talked about this for a long time," Margaret Truman yelled over Ogy! Orgy! Orgy!. To Hell with pussy footing around. This is our time."

Later, members would recall the inspirational words, the transfigured look upon the face of Truman, the ripping of cloth. After the initial excitement the o.c was formed and sprung immediately into action.

"Estimates are from thirty to forty reporters here right now. Almost all men."

"What do we do with the women?"

"Are you crazy? We invite them!!!"

"They don't have anything we want."

"Okay. Leave them out."

"What about that reporter from the Sun?"

"He's pretty cute."

"No! Not him. We're having fresh meat."

"Belinda Bardahl – reserve the rec room for tomorrow night."

"What if it's taken?"

"Wednesday night everybody'll be dancing to the band at Humpter Landing. Everybody but us that is."

It was decided to fan out into the community. When they spotted a reporter one committee member would invite him to meet her there for a juicy tidbit of news. Reporters never would pass on to their competitors this opportunity so each would be expecting an exclusive. Each would be in for a surprise. Beverages and snacks would be laid out on a table. Lighting would be dimmed.

"We tell them to be there at 6:30, the door will be unlocked. We may need tables. Lots of tables. Everybody bring a table," was declared amid a chorus of giggles. "Strong ones."

Violent injury and death in The Villages occur almost exclusively at the many car shows. Occasionally a man will be gazing under the hood of a GTO wondrously devoid of anti pollution hoses, computers, fuel injectors and plastic fluid reservoirs. Battery to motor to radiator. What was wrong with that combo? The space, the very space in there to work on an engine, change your own spark plugs, true elbow room, a man can crawl in there and never come out. "I'll have dinner by the exhaust manifold, dear." As the old feelings of points and carburation flood back into him with their youthful associations, another worshiper leans in and knocks out the hood support, carburetor- face and broken back the most common complaints, depending on the hood.

Bud Anderson was salivating over a Chevy 409, *I Get Around* droning in his head, considering licking the shiny orange paint on the valve covers. Suddenly a strong hand was pushing down on the back of Anderson's neck giving him air cleaner face with the other hand on the hood-support rod.

"Hey. Lemmee go," emerged a muffled whimper.

"I might let the hood go if I don't get some straight answers from you, dirtbag."

A muffled "Who are you?" followed.

"I'm the guy can drop this hood on you."

"Is he alright?" a car buff asked.

"Yeah. He just wants to look real close. I'm helping him."

"Hmm. What are ya seeing there, buddy?"

"He's concentrating too hard to answer. He thinks if he looks close enough for long enough, he can see into the engine. Like Superman."

"Well, not really. Superman didn't have to get close. Or even try. He could use his x-ray vision."

"I don't think Superman wasted x-ray vision on seeing through no engine."

"No, he'd usually just look through walls and stuff."

Muffled cries rose from the air cleaner. "Hey. He musta made it. Me, I wouldn't be looking through walls either. More likely stuff'."

"Okay – see ya, pal. I just spotted my first car."

"Yeah goodbye. Okay, Anderson. You just tell me where you were on April the tenth, the day before they found Beasley's poor sad body with all the fun he was gonna have stolen right out of it. Then I want to know where you were on the day they found him. Take your time. I got all minute."

Anderson farted organically. "Oh Christ. You son-of-a-bitch, you try that again, I'll drop this hood and the hell with you. I oughta punch you for doin' that to me." More muffled sounds rose from the engine.

"Time's up. And no more talkin' out your ass."

Buz Murdock strolled up chewing gum. "Hey man, what's happening here? It doesn't look cool."

"Mind your own business wise guy."

Henry Fondue joined Murdock. "Hangin's every man's business."

"Yeah Daddio."

"I got two hands. You wanta join this guy here under the hood?"

Murdock backed off. "I'm cool."

Fondue wasn't quite sure what he was doing there anyway and sat on a bench.

"You got your answers ready Anderson?"

"Mmff."

"Alright. You can come on out."

"Swell."

"Why'd you kill Joe Beasley?"

"What??!? Who's Joe Beasley?"

"You don't even know who he was and you killed him? I oughta end you right now, scum."

"Hold on. I don't know him and I *didn't* kill him."

"That's better. Don't worry. I'm askin' everybody in case I get lucky."

"You a policeman?"

"Don't worry about that. You just worry about April the tenth and where you were."

"Excuse me," Eddie Haskel, the head of Car Show Promotions and Custom Cremation, said to Barney Jenkins. "I don't mean to cause you inconvenience, sir, but holding people down under the hood of a car is not a sanctioned activity at our shows."

Jenkins looked at Haskel like he was stunned that such a person actually would speak and reveal himself. "I got no idea what that has to do with me. Bud, do you know what this creep's talking about?"

"No, I guess not."

"Oh, I'm not chastising you for doing it," said Haskel smiling. "I'm just letting people know it's not okay and if they see such activity they should call the police."

That was all the excuse the ex-cop needed to put Haskel under the hood but he held back, trying to learn from similar events that had not helped his prematurely over career. "Yeah, yeah, sure. I'll keep my eye out." He took out his glass eye. "See?"

On observing this an elderly woman fainted, banging her head on the driver side rear view mirror on her way down. Haskel phoned for paramedics as Bud Anderson said, "See ya," to Jenkins and headed to the malt shop where the waitress already was flirting with Buz Murdock.

Buz flashed her a quick grin.

"You have great teeth," she said. "I suppose you hear that all the time."

"Yeah. I inherited them from my grandfather."

"You can't beat good genes."

"No, I really inherited these choppers from my grandfather. Pop got them first and he handed them down to me, I got them implanted when he died."

"Oh," the waitress said. "They do look good."

"Best ever. They beat the ones I had and really, what better way to honor Gramps? He's still chewing the fat."

Murdock noticed Bud Anderson lurking around. "Hey – sit down kid. What's that guy's beef?"

"Thanks for the help, Mr. Cool."

"I tried. I don't know you. Maybe you had it coming. I ain't seen your road map; where you been, where you're going."

"Cut the crap, Buz. I thought you were tough."

45

"Sometimes tough ain't enough. He knew I had my eye out for him."

"Oh yeah. I just saw what that means and you come up way short."

"Oh yeah?" Buz pulled out his right eye.

"For the love of Mike," Anderson wailed. "Can everybody do that?"

"Maybe you can," Murdock consoled him, putting back his eye. "Try it."

"I don't think I will, Buz. I'm too afraid I can."

"Are you gonna sit down?"

The bobby-socked waitress was back. "Who's your friend?"

"Oh, this is one of those cats from under the hood. A real motorhead."

"Very funny Buz."

"I've never seen you two around here before."

"We're probably new in town," Buz rejoined enigmatically.

"Well," Dotty said. "I think I have the liberty of inviting you to an event coming soon. You definitely qualify. I've had my eye on you since you came in."

"Nope, that's it," Bud said, heading for the door. "I'm out of here. Why not take your nose off while you're at it?"

Buz watched him go then looked at Dotty and shrugged. "He's a little excitable. Now what about this event?"

7

Emboldened by recent political developments, the Ku Kux Klan had relocated from Taft, Florida to Lady Lake. Their office window sported a modest sign reading 'AMERIKINS FOR A BETTER TRUMP'. As they waited for somebody to notice, a conflab ensued among the steering committee. "We fin'ly git one in the Black House and what do he do but set there and do nothin', in the middle of Jews?!?"

"I know, Curtis. Next thing he'll probly get rid of old Ivodka and marry a nigger."

"Good one Ty. Ivodka. How'd you come up with that?"

"Ain't that her name?"

"Never mind. I thought you made up a joke."

Buddy Burnsed Chimed in. "What about him sayin, 'There's fine people on both sides?' What kinda dog-doo is that?"

"It's bull dog-doo is what is it." Wayne Wagner put an RC Cola to his thin lips. "He was in there four years. I ain't seen one 'whites only' sign."

"That's right," Buddy considered. "Not even a drinkin' fountain."

"His daddy'd be rollin around in his grave"

"Nothin's changed, Wayne," Curtis clarified. "It just ain't. Jews still runnin' the worl', jigs still runnin' the Jews, Kathlicks ever'where you look. It's depressin'".

"Shoot. We even got Kathlick niggers."

Curtis shook his head. "I don't even know what to make of that."

"Why'd he even bother bein' pres'dent?"

"You'd think he was president of Mexico the way he's allus carryin on about Mexicans."

"You know what?" Ty Wiggins put in. "I don't even think he's racist."

This elicited an outpouring of opposition. "Jest listen," Wiggins said, trying to quell the mob. "He mighta acted like he was to git our vote."

"No way. His daddy was in the Klan," said Burnsed."

"Well that don't mean he has to be. Mebbe he didn't respeck his daddy."

Curtis sighed. "It's so frustratin'. When we wins we still loses. Mebbe we kin at least git somethin' did over here in Them Villages. We knows them folks believes in the cause."

"Well sure they do. But it ain't their lookout. They ain't got nobody botherin 'em there. They's okay. Screw the Klan."

48

Wayne Clewless perked up. "I got it! I got it!"

There was a group groan. "What Wayne?"

"You know how they's allus havin' bands and what-not Satiddy night in Them Villages ?"

"Yeah Wayne."

"Let's have a lynchin."

There was a collective sigh. "We cain't have no lynchin' in Them Villages, Wayne."

Buddy Burnsed raised his hand. "Yeah, Buddy."

"Wayne might be onto somethin' fer oncet. It could be pretend, like a play or somethin'."

Clewless jumped up. "I knows what 'pretend' means Buddy. Why would ennybody come to a pretend lynchin'? We git us a real nigger and we strings 'im up. He starts out alive and ends up dead."

"Now where we gonna get one o' them to hang these days, Wayne? Even if we tricks him into showin' up, he'd put up such a howl like you never heerd when he figured out what we's up to. And these days, that's all it'd take."

"Mebbe he won't figure out 'til it's too late."

"Wayne," Curtis Baumgardner said, exasperated, "they ain't no nigger that stupid."

"Well, we could pay 'im."

Wayne Wagner jumped back in. "Wayne, can you just tell us where he figures he'll spend the money after we hang 'im?"

"I don't know. I ain't a nigger. Mebbe he'll get hisself a nice pine box."

"But don't you see, Wayne? If he sez no, he won't need no money fer no pine box 'cause he'll still be alive. So he'll have the same amount of money. And, fer a bonus, he won't get lynched."

"Well yeah, but then he'd need money fer other stuff."

"Alright, Wayne," Baumgardner said. "Good idea. If we sold tickets we'd probly get rich. So we'll think about it."

"Alright."

"Curtis," Burnsed added, Clewless having aroused nostalgia, "we could put up a poster in the window, jest see what folks sez. If they gets all mad we can say we was just funnin.'"

"You know Donald Trump might hear about it and say somethin'."

"It would probly get on computers."

8

Maxine Falderall was sitting up in bed with the latest issue of *The Villages Daily Sun.* "Heloise always knows just what to say, don't you think so Jimmy?"

"I sure do," said the paper's rising star. "What does she say today?"

"She says always wave to drivers who do you a kindness on the road."

"If everybody read Heloise's column," Oldson said while spreading a deep layer of pineapple flavored cream cheese on the butter already soaking into his toasted onion bagel, "the world would sure be a nicer place."

"It's because a woman wrote that she waved thank you with her open hand but wasn't sure the kind driver understood. Heloise said that was just the right signal to send."

"What else does Heloise say?" Jimmy asked with a mouthful.

"Well, she offers a labeling tip. It's very clever."

"What is it my dear?"

"Heloise says to put red or purple nail polish on keys, the Off position on appliances and guess what the third one is."

"Being an investigative reporter, I shall begin the process of deduction. The pattern I see is these are all things that must be located. Am I right?"

Maxine nodded.

"I know what it is. And there's not a moment to lose." He dug the nail polish from Maxine's purse. "It's gold but it'll have to do," he said, applying a tiny dot to her forehead."

"Now you won't lose me," she said giggling.

"Thank goodness for Heloise."

Jimmy Oldson kissed Maxine a loving good-bye. "You gonna be alright?"

"Better than I've ever been," she said.

Maxine gazed at him moon-eyed as he headed out to do his job: inflating mundane human stuff to fill up the newspaper with.

"Don't forget there might be a murderer loose out there," she fretted.

"I'll be alright," he assured her. "I can take care of myself. Just remember to keep the door locked and don't let anyone in."

Oldson spotted two reporters lurking around his apartment. "Look fellas," he said, "there's nothing to see here. I'm just a reporter. Maxine Falderall has placed herself in seclusion at an undisclosed location until the baby is born."

"Who's Maxine Underalls? We heard Bigfoot was living here."

"Yeah, yeah and, and Putin. Yeah, he's supposed to be around."

"Very funny, guys. But you're not going to find either one of them here. You might as well go home and wait for the next installment in *The Sun.*"

"We might just hang around and see what turns up."

"Suit yourselves but it sounds pretty boring to me."

"I don't mind. I got something happening later on."

"Yeah, me too."

The reporters looked at each other suspiciously.

Like Oldson, many people employed in The Villages actually reside in the nearby, far cheaper and less restrictive Lady Lake. They're known to Villagers as "Outlyers." They shop, dine, fart, stroll, see movies and dance to the music of The Villages; then as the final notes of the band trail off into the ether the charade ends and they step into their pumpkins and motor back home, smug in enjoying the best of both worlds. If age appropriate, to the unpracticed eye they look like Villageers. Further camouflaging them is the itinerant nature of most Villageers who reside there only in winter. Villageers take pride in being able to spot the interlopers. Exiting or entering an actual car often is the first clue to their identity, savvy interlopers parking obscurely. A woman dating one will be shunned if discovered, just as if she were dating a Democrat, which for a few mavericks injects an element of daring and

Shakespeare. However it is tacitly acceptable for Villages men to accommodate outlying women as long as they don't overdo it, the community temporarily turning a blind eye.

Snowbirds may be either demeaned or exalted. Like Alaskans who respect only those who endure winter, year round Villageers claim primacy over those who skip summer. On the other hand snowbirds tend to be better heeled, including some minor celebrities.

Because of all this, Lady Lake was on Oldson's beat. As he walked the limited streets, his reporter's eye noticed many reporter-like men aimlessly posted here and there, drinking coffee, reading the sports page, looking at their phones, seeming like men biding their time. Then he noticed a new store front. "This could be a few lines," he thought, as always.

Oldson pushed open the vinyl door to find Wayne Clueless minding the store. "What's this about getting a better Trump?" he cheerfully asked Clewless who was leaning back behind the table with his feet up.

Wayne plopped forward and looked squint-eyed at Oldson. "Who're you? A communiss dictator?"

Oldson laughed. "No, just a reporter. Whatcha got going on here? Don't like the Trump we had?"

"What's it to you?"

"Like I said I'm a reporter. Don't you want to talk to a reporter? Get the word out?"

"I think you should get the *Hell* out. Whaddayou think of that, Mr. Conkrite?"

"My name's Oldson. Jimmy Oldson. Here's my card."

"Nice card."

Oldson returned it to his pocket. "Is there anybody else here I can talk to?"

"We're havin' a lynchin."

Jimmy smiled. "Okay. Now we're talking. When's this luncheon going to be?"

Wayne leaned back and looked sideways again. "You thinks that's a good idea, do ya?"

"We don't have a lot going on here so, you bet."

"Well gollee. Wait til I tell the boys about this."

Jimmy had out his pad and pencil. "Now when and where?"

"Oh, we ain't decided yet."

"You can give me a call when you know."

"We's gonna put up a sign in the window. You come back and read it there. It'll be soon. Y'all got any niggers around here?"

"No," said Oldson, "I don't think we do."

"Run 'em all off?"

"I don't really know."

"Well, local's allus better. But the sooner you kin git us one the sooner we kin git on with it."

"I'm a reporter, not a job recruiter."

"Any white wimmen git forced around here lately?"

"Not that I know of."

"Thought you wuz a reporter. Git along now Conkrite." Clewless made a brooming gesture toward the door with his hand.

On that note Oldson left, assuming he had been speaking to a half-wit just watching the office. "This is an unusual form of affirmative action," he thought. "Might be a paragraph or two in it. I can't wait to come back and see who'll be here next."

9

ince John Smith had been expelled from the many Villages softball teams he was on, he sat at home a lot more watching reruns, familiarity breeding contempt for him and his colostomy. Pocahontas was looking beyond her domestic horizon, specifically toward the evening's Woman's Club "Get-together." While her husband watched 12 year-old Beaver act like he still was six, with his now eighteen year old brother Wally noticing nothing developmentally wrong because he was still twelve, she planned her entrance into the meeting. When all were present and at the food table, Margaret Truman would announce her as the keynote speaker. Once she had heard the doors locking, she would cartwheel across the stage, losing her minimal clothing as she went. Then she would disappear briefly, then reappear at floor level and saunter down into the crowd as Truman dimmed the lights. She would clear a space on the table and sit there with her legs crossed. Just see what would happen next. Presumably the other members would follow suit, maybe one at a time. Everyone will start with their gold slippers, walk over and line them up against the wall, then walk back, just standing there barefoot or in stockings. What would the reporters be thinking then.

She herself would make no move toward any man, just hand out horse douvres from her position, maybe mix a drink or two, very congenial. What are reporters like? I hope they're not stuffed shirts. I hope they're charming and adventurous. And without bags. Well anyway it goes, it will be a night to remember. She smiled a little.

"Tonight? Is tonight the night you go to the Woman's Club? I thought this was Bingo night."

"Call it that if you like."

You know we haven't had a nice night together, just the two us, in a long time."

"We never did. You were always playing softball so you never noticed."

"Oh yeah. Those were the days."

"So whadaya say tonight we hunker down, eat in, do a jigsaw. Like I thought we used to do."

"You just hold onto that evening and we'll have it real soon." She tweaked his nose, threw a scarf across her shoulders and headed for the door. "But not tonight."

One could well imagine that, as with most wild schemes, the conspirators individually chickened out, leaving 35 reporters from various outlets and papers across the country with only one woman to interview, sitting nude crosslegged on the empty food table; that when it came right down to it, middle-aged desperate woman can be reined in by some atrophied impulses toward decency and decorum and turn away from Sodom and Gomorrah. Or that they did all trickle in but straight-laced and ready to defend their honor in the face of whatever challenges presented themselves to it. It might have been a nice meet-and-greet for some lonely bored men far away from home. One of these scenarios might have prevailed but as it were, the event took on a life of its own, the membership of The Villages Woman's Club arriving almost trance-like. A crowd of reporters who felt wronged and duped by each other's arrival at the exclusive interview- turned press conference was nonetheless lured inside by the promise of free food and drinks. They grumbled loudly as Margaret Truman ascended the diaz watching a wary Buz Murdock walk through the doorway last. After a generic greeting from Truman, the ka-chink of doors locking signaled the next act. Soon reporters were nonplussed by the rotating Pocahontas Smith juggernauting across the stage like the giant hubcap of nudity, flimsy clothes flying asunder. Lights dimmed during Smith's sultry stroll down the stairs and toward the food table, led by a bush blasting out like Pomp and Circumstance number1. The men of the press became silent, each aware that something special may be in the offing. And so they stayed, every last one of them, including Buz Murdock.

Arriving home that evening with tales of his interesting time working, Jimmy Oldson was dismayed to realize Maxine was not there waiting for him.

"Oh I met all the reporters," she informed him on returning – "Womans Club meet and greet. They never suspected who I was. I don't think they were paying much attention to people's faces anyway."

Next day bleary eyed reporters hunched over coffee cups having sworn each other to secrecy, readying themselves for an exit, some considering attending a church some day soon. Buz Murdock was escorted by Margaret Truman to his dilapidated Corvette and cardinals still were able to tweet.

PART 2

10

As the semi-monthly Donald Trump Memory Parade was assembling, and paramedics began lining the route, Jimmy the Geek was counting participants and making the line on how many Villageers wouldn't cross the finish line and how many would require aid from a paramedic along the way. A separate bet was how many would die trying. The Geek was at a table outside Johnny Rocket's surveying the pack, tallying the oxygen tanks. He noted only a few this time, indicative of either a die-off or high humidity. Usually nobody actually died en-route so the Geek was giving pretty good odds. To "die" a participant had to fall and be dead in the parade route. Dying later somewhere else didn't pay off, even on the sidewalk. To name the casualty was "win", to guess the number of perished was "place," and "show" was to call that there would be death.

"Barry – Why don't you do the walk? Make things interesting."

The Croation leaned back, indignant. "You think I

can't make it?"

"That's not what I'm talking about. Lots of 'em won't make it past Dunkin' Donuts. I'm saying you won't survive it. You'll make it to the end alright but it won't be the end of the parade."

"Yeah? Here's a sawbuck says I will."

"Is life that cheap to you? You know how much people that ain't alive would pay to be alive? Just for an hour? And you're willing to throw away at least a good month or two for ten bucks?" (There are, it seems a lot of hucksters in the land of the dead, offering a trip back to life of varying durations. Lack of funds would be a problem but the hucksters aren't in it for the money, useless to them anyway. And they never grant the wish, thriving on the futile desperation of dead people presented with a shot, however brief, of the good old days.)

The Croation slurped his vanilla milk shake. "It's worth it just to prove you wrong."

"Save it for a sunny day. You know you can't bet on yourself. You can walk. You just can't walk and bet. I'm not going to be your life insurance."

"I'm not doing it for free. Just between me and you. Here. I'll make it twenty."

The Geek shook his head. "I can't factor in any of this. You walk and die because of our bet, changes the payoff. It's like insider trading. My reputation's shot. It's all I got. Ain't no "between you and me." Anyway, what about Angie? You thought about her? You die for The Donald she goes on the market. Ooh lala."

"You're such an ?*!hole."

"You know I've always had a thing for her. Maybe I should take the bet."

"She's never gone in for dwarfs. Anyway it's in my will – you get within fifty feet of her she loses everything."

The Geek sighed. "Barry, you got a lot to live for. Never forget that."

"Looks like the optimists are pretty much assembled," the Croation alerted the Geek.

"Yeah, I got my tally. Look - there's some new guys – Americans for a Better Trump. Ooh. I don't know how that's gonna play."

"There's Jim Baxter and Brunch Rickey goin' over there."

"Now they're laughin' and shakin' hands. Must have past mustard somehow."

"Doesn't sound like a bad idea to me. A better Trump would be less like Trump."

"You better not say that too loud. I don't wanta pay off *your* odds."

"I'm touched."

With the exodus of the press corps Jimmy Oldson and Maxine Falderall were free to mingle with the public, frequently taking walks around Lake Humpter Village, their favorite. Whatever fancy Maxine's appetite took, they could satisfy it there. Reactions to the couple were tantamount to a white man and a black woman. Some looked away, some thought terrible thoughts and others greeted them pleasantly. All were uncomfortable.

"Jimmy," Maxine said, "You got any good stories cooking?"

"Well, now that you mention it, doing a piece right now on John Smith getting kicked out of softball."

"Tell me more. Tell me more."

"It's developing into quite a tale of deceit and intrigue overseen by the love of the game."

"Yes?"

"Okay, I start the story with 'There's three bags in softball – first, second and third. There's no colostomy bag. But John Smith didn't see it that way. For the last year and a half he put the fourth bag in the field."

Maxine viewed the cub reporter with adoration. "That's wonderful."

Jimmy blushed and looked away. "Thanks."

"Any leads in your murder case?"

"No hot leads but there's an awful lot of possibilities out there."

"No suspects," she asked coyly, squeezing his hand.

"Well, I met this really crabby guy, says he knew the victim, certainly seemed mean enough to kill someone."

"What about me? What if I did it?"

"Being an objective reporter, I haven't ruled that possibility out. But you wouldn't kill somebody, would you?"

"Oh, no. Heaven forbid."

Suddenly a couple hundred Villageers have something besides a beer belly growing in their front, women and men. On closer inspection it turns out they're all with child.

Maxine was the first to present her product, the process made unusual by the infant crying all the way out. But nothing could prepare the medical team for what emerged. The delivery doctor recoiled in horror as the orange hair and face of Donald Trump was gradually revealed, as welcome as a slow motion hot dog growing out the top of your head. It was an eight pound replica of the former president, not as he would have looked as a baby but as he looked at present, naked.

Nobody wanted to touch it as it lay on the table kicking and screaming until its mother reached down and pulled it to her breast where it immediately knew what to do. Primitive thoughts of dispatching the infant rose in the minds of onlookers. Sensing this, Jimmy Oldson rose to its defense.

"Hey now, wait a minute. This is my baby. I don't know how the heck it came out looking like that, but I'm going to love it with all my heart and hope that it grows into something else."

Just then it seemed the baby was trying to say something to Maxine but it fell back into silence.

The doctor shrugged his shoulders, removed his mask and walked out the room muttering something about medical school, perhaps to join the French Foreign Legion. Jimmy's mother similarly shrugged her shoulders with resignation and the whole ridiculous turn her life had recently taken and left, saying "See ya," on her way through the doorway.

Back at the apartment an air of solemnity and an inkling of dread replaced the anticipation Jimmy Oldson and Maxine had felt. Jimmy looked at her suspiciously. "You didn't, I mean, you and Trump did..."

"Jimmy!"

"Alright, alright. Maybe it's just a weird resemblance. Babies are usually ugly at first, right?"

"Yes, that's right," Maxine agreed optimistically.

"But not that ugly."

Maxine burst into tears.

In a Pygmy village deep in the Congo, where no white man has been, pregnancies began terminating in teeny-weeny Donald Trumps. They were killed immediately and bar-b-qued.

As other female pregnancies came to fruition in The Villages, the pattern became clear. An entire race of Donald Trump had been spawned. The Florida anti-abortion law, while making exception for alien abduction said nothing about post menopausal or male pregnancies likely to result in a former President. Yet none desired to opt out from this mass experience and connection to Trump. Overnight a new American Bethlehem had risen. Not kings with frankincense and myrrh, but a vast American herd converged on the sacred setting to view Frankenstein and her. The country's economy verged on collapse as men and women turned from their minimum wage jobs to be swept into the flood. To avert the crisis a national holiday was declared.

Most scientists, wanting time to concoct an explanation, were at a loss. Tv preachers also were eerily silent. "I'm guessing, and this is only a guess," cautioned Dr. Phil, "he's such a presence there, well, his essence must have literally been absorbed by the population."

The affected men began to "show," eventually developing breasts and releasing through the bowels fully formed replicas of Don Junior. No scientists stepped forth to explain this.

Jimmy the Geek, feeling he was beginning to crown, was rubbing his hands together. "I could make a mint selling these things," he schemed. "Especially to Europeans. They'd go nuts over 'em."

The biblical Maxine's time in the spotlight was limited as other female pregnancies came to fruition with the same result. The first male to produce one, dubbed "the Virgin Marvin" became an instant sensation on YouHoo, holding up the little shit in the bathroom by one leg. Other male pregnancies were found gurgling and screaming in the toilet, having exited with no more umbilical chord than poop had. Several were inadvertently flushed but that only clogged the commode and the newborns were safely tugged out.

Some of the remaining pregnant villageers, mostly non-Republicans, petitioned for termination, but likelihood of a baby becoming a Republican was judged by the Republican Florida Supreme Court an inadequate criterion for abortion. Differing opinions abounded, but largely from the scientific community. Trump himself threatened an executive order to prohibit termination but he was no longer president.

Among theologians the debate raged over whether or not each infant had a soul, one composite soul or no soul at all, like the original. The Pope said lack of a soul in the original would render the point moot.

"Well, Jimmy," Maxine ventured with a coy look, "it looks like I'm not so special after all."

Jimmy sat beside Maxine on the purple couch he was going to throw away when the Lantana money came in and drew her to him. "You're special alright. And you were the first. Speaking of that, where's little Trumpy now?"

"He's taking a nap. Jimmy, they wouldn't come and take him from me ... would they?"

"Who, my love?"

"Well, you know, his family."

"There is talk of quarantining the Villages until they make sure it's not contagious."

"Oh Jimmy, it's just so crazy. Our little baby..."

"I know, Maxine. I know."

For six months The Villages was quarantined, no further pregnancies of any sort impinging on the population, isolation disrupting but little the routine of most Villageers. The FDA explained it as a one-off Lamarkian phenomenon where the group unconsciousness was focused so intensely that manifestations were spontaneously generated in any available human cavity. It was noted that dog and cat pregnancies had proceeded at the usual rate with no anomalies, although one litter of Rottweilers was said to resemble Donald Trump's daughter-in-law.

Now of course, the main question was what to do with them. Keep it as your child or a pet? None considered giving them up for adoption. The legality of selling them was debated with no resolution. For a little breathing room and to feed the delusion that everything was just fine and normal enough, Donald Trump pre-school was established. Parents were strongly encouraged to enroll their odious offspring and the doors opened to two-hundred fifty of them. They had to wear identity bracelets so parents could tell whose was whose although many didn't really care as long as they got one back after school was out. A class action lawsuit was initiated by Jimmy the Geek to force the Trump family to pay for food and clothing. The suit was handled by the local firm *Morgan and Morgan and Morgan and Morgan, ad infinitum,* who could relate to the situation.

"Things are going just as you predicted," Agzorf bloofed to Gleeep in their native language from below the Earth's crust and directly under The Villages.

"Yes. We will expand the program and the next generation of meat will all be Donald Trump, big and fat. Then we initiate the harvest."

"Yes, by then we should have the process perfected."

So – it turns out the race of beings occupying the antecrustial layer of Earth are the biggest boosters of Donald Trump ever, mainly because he is big and fat.

Subterraneans like Agzorf and Gleeep are great scientists compared to humans but they know only one motivation – hunger. And the other thing is how to satisfy it. Not a ruminative bunch, the residents of the crust and below survive by exclusively focusing on the thing they need to do – eat. All else, such as subjects humans discourse on, seems to take care of itself. Pickings are slim where they live and they get but fleeting glimpses of the abundant surface world and in one of those glimpses Gleeep saw Donald Trump at a rally. Never had he imagined anything so delectable and he and Agzorf invented the translateral incubator beam, which reads molecules and then impregnates people with them. They still hadn't worked out how to get these morsels down there but they counted on lots of time for that.

Meanwhile Donald Trump released a pre-recorded Fox News interview regarding all his duplicates. Adopting a philosophical aspect, Trump turned to the left and started to speak but then stopped and turned the other way reengaging his speech process. "Do you suppose," he posed, "anyone has ever found a needle in a haystack? No. But they hold it out there, don't they? Even you may some day find a needle. The American dream. That's what they say. Any American may some day find a needle in a haystack. Is it a heroin needle? A tweedle needle? I don't know.

"You're not going to, you know. Nobody is ever going to. Who would look for a needle in a haystack anyway? I'm asking you. Would you? Wouldn't it be better to look in a box of needles? Maybe Joltin' Joe would. He might. He'd never find it. Nope, he never would. He might find

71

other needles but not the one he's looking for. Even if he did, he'd never tell anybody. Just so he could keep looking for that needle."

Trump paused to let his words be absorbed by Americans. "I could. I could find one if I wanted to. And when I did, I'd tell the American people."

Asked, "Why do you think all these babies of you happened?" Trump replied, "I don't really know. Divine providence or something like that. I don't know. Are there enough for every non-shithole country to have one as president? Maybe. Then I could be president of the whole worthwhile world. Wouldn't that be something?" The ex-president trailed off.

"As president of the WWW, do you think you could make Earth great again?"

Trump scowled a little. "I'm not making any predictions on that. There's a lot wrong with some parts of Earth that aren't very great and they never were great. We'll just have to wait and see."

"Do you feel envious of people who have these babies when you don't?"

Trump struck a thoughtful pose. "It's a perfect opportunity for revenge. Maybe I'll buy one and give it to Don Junior to raise. See how he likes it. I have thought I might like to buy a few back and freeze them in case something happens to the other ones. So we'll always have proof when people way beyond the future, way out there far, so far, try to say this never happened." Like Gandhi. You know they froze Gandhi don't you? So he'll always be there. Great man. What a great guy, made South America great again... And Willie Mays. Yeah I think they froze him too." Trump shrugs. "I don't know exactly why... Did they freeze Willie? Does anybody know that for sure?"

11

Nothing can be astonishing for very long. It stays around awhile, slipping into the mundane. As things settled back to normal, albeit a new one, Jimmy Oldson returned to his search for the ender of Joe Beasley. But the trail, never hot, had gone colder.

For Villageers requiring a refined search in their randy quest, merely gold slippers provides too little detail. Once having homed in on the shoes, Valentino has to stealthily track her to the golf cart where the color-coded loofah flag would reveal how to proceed and what to expect; from white for "I'm shy" to red for "Grab me by the pussy" to polka dotted for "What are you waiting for?" Publix bag-codger is the supremely coveted part-time job because they know everybody's code. Without that you're on your own. In a bar and feeling lucky, you'll go straight for the crotch and if she says, "Oh, Hello Donald," you know you're in. Bag-codger Jimmy the Geek does a lively trade with the closest thing to a dating service The Villages has, correlating data and selling it to those frustrated by failing eyesight or always too far away to make out the loofah. Bignoculars per capita are in The Villages more than any other spot on Earth, bird watching having caught on in a big way. As for the blind, they just feel their way around and something good eventually happens.

Then there are the women required by social mores to travel without loofah. These are the infamous "Black Widows," the ones who have taken lives in bed. Two notorious ones, nicknamed Calamity Jane and Annie Croakley, had scored numerous times. No loofah but notches inside the door.

The Villages was abuzz like a buzzer factory with the news that the reinstater of American greatness himself would preside over the next Trump Day Parade. The great day arrived and Trump's personal convertible car cruised slowly up Lake Humpter Road, Secret Service walking alongside gorging on Big Macs given them free by the former president. Trump did the Miss America wave and delighted the crowd with hilarious imitations of any handicapped people he could spot along the route. Villageers lined both sides with the usual signs, chanting "You'll wonder where Joe Biden went when you brush your teeth with Pepsodent." As the motorcade passed they held out their little trumpsters in tiny Trump suits. This is what the original was here for. No man can be prepared for the impact of such a thing, let alone a narcissist: a gauntlet entirely of oneself. It seemed to Trump that each baby, as it saw him, fell immediately in love with its template. Soon it was like traveling through the aorta of bliss with pure viscous love mushrooms impinging on him from all sides and spraying out of every orifice on Kim Jong Un's plump, naked body. He wished the Korean dictator could have been there with him so he too could witness the all-encompassing adoration. The Donald had to go beyond just seeing it. He needed to feel it. Stepping from the car, Trump lay on the street on his back and yelled, "Come on."

Soon Donald Trump was entirely immersed in himself. When it was over, no one expected to get back his own baby but that didn't matter. They had become as one.

At Confuckius' Chinese Barbeque, Jimmy Oldson glanced at the boring black shoes of the customer walking in the door, then returned to unfurling his fortune, hoping for something romantic to show Maxine. The cookie contents read, You'll wonder where Joe Beasley went when you brush your teeth with Mike Pence.

"Nothing romantic about that," the disappointed star reporter and 1/3 owner of the Villages Sun thought. "But wait a minute... that's an awfully specific fortune cookie. Maybe this is a clue. All those Mike Pence look-alikes out there. I thought it was a new fad, but – what if it was just Mike Pence walking around? What if Trump sent him here to take out Beasely freeing up women for him when he came around? What if Mike Pence is just here having a big time while pretending to be a Mike Pence look-alike? Gee willikers, what a story that would be...

12

ike Pence accepted another triple root beer float from his Tunisian slave girl, and ordered a little Zamfir, then laid back in his elephant-stomach bathtub, warm high fructose corn syrup flooding his every inch, ready to relax. "Those were the days," Pence reminisced, "raping and pillaging across Africa, me and God. The times we had." A smile cracked his pasty face as he recalled the time God cornered two rhinos and a pygmy and then wrestled them into submission. "And the pygmy gave Him the hardest time. Kept getting away and kicking God in the nuts and stuff, seemed like God couldn't see him very well. What a hoot. And the women. Wow! God's over there trying to pull up a tree or something, attracting a crowd and I had them all to myself. Good old God, not much interested in human women but you show Him a nice piece of elephant or even a giraffe! 'I'll show you what that neck is for, Pence,' He said that time just before showing me. Killed the giraffe but that was sure something to see. Woowee He went for them. He said it's because human women look too much like Him, would make Him feel almost like a homo if He went with one. Then He tried to make me do a little hippo. God says, 'Just give it a try, Pence. Why not?' I really didn't want to do it, in case somebody saw me.

"I said, 'It's against my religion.' To look at God then, you'd have to believe that was the funniest thing He'd ever heard. Took Him a couple months to recover. I just left and came back.

"He says, 'Oh there you are. Good one.' But I was glad I did that for Him because usually I didn't contribute much, just a hanger-on. I remember wondering a little why He even bothered with me.

"What about the day we're flying around in a tornado and I asked Him did He ever wish He didn't make us in His image but He just looked at me like that was the dumbest thing He ever heard. He said, 'So then I got nothing in My image. Just a bunch of animals that don't look like Me running around. Is that what you're suggesting, Pence? Nobody to root for? Nobody to mess with? I wanted that, I could just go to one of those other planets, couldn't I?'

"That's when I started keeping my ideas to myself a little more. I almost asked Him if He could really go to other planets. That could have been really bad. I don't know if He even knew what sex they were half the time. Don't know if He cared... how about the time He knocked up an elephant. That was something. We got back to the zoo just in time to see the result come out. Whoowee! That was the *real* elephant man. Its mother wasn't impressed, that's for sure. What a look God got; like 'this is what I've been carrying around for the last twenty-two months?!?' I said to God, 'The next Messiah?' That was another time I wished I'd kept my mouth shut. But I think I know what He was thinking – 'No way we're getting *that* on a cross in thirty years.' Reminds me of when I asked if in the good old days He'd ever given it to a tyrannosaurus, just making idle conversation. Pass the time, you know? Again God just looked at me.

"'Pence,' He said, 'I'm beginning to think you may be the stupidest person I ever made. Have you *seen* a tyrannosaurus?' And I said well no, I hadn't and that set Him on a tear about fossils.

"I loved it when we used to sneak into Hell, kind of a reconnaissance mission. I wasn't allowed to see how we got there so I had to keep my eyes shut at first. Now that was interesting. *Phew!* I never could entirely relax because I was always a little bit worried God would forget and leave without me. I certainly had no idea where the exit was. After one of those visits, me and God are just kind of lying around in the Mississippi River and God comes over all thoughtful and disturbed, a little storm cloud even formed over His groin. He looks at me and says 'You know, Mike (I always knew something was up when He called me that, like it wasn't me anymore, could have been any of a billion Mikes, didn't matter. Shoot. He could have been talking to Mike Maguire. I almost refused to listen but I'm glad I didn't.) 'Mike,' He says to every Mike in the world, 'I could have been anything I wanted. Anything. I had tons of potential.' Then He grabbed me by the shoulders and looked me straight in the eye and said, 'I could have been Somebody, Mike. Where'd it all go? I ask you.'

"I took a stab at it. 'You made the universe. That was pretty good.'"

"'Like I said, Mike,' He replied with an air of impatience, 'I could have done anything. I might have worked in concepts, not things. You want to make the universe, you make a bunch of things, natural law takes over and bam! There it is. Now what? You know why I never gave it to a tyrannosaurus? Because there never were any tyrannosauruses. Or any triceratopses or anything else like that. Why would I make dinosaurs when there were no people to have to deal with them and I wasn't supposed to make people for another couple hundred million years and I just couldn't wait and I made the people first. Gave you fossils for perspective, make everybody think I made dinosaurs and I might make them again if you don't toe the line, all for the glory. Hell. *You* could have made fossils. I'm a lot closer to you, Mike, than to what I could have Been.' He just looked at me, at a loss for further words, then slowly turned away. If only He had confided that to just me and not Mikes in general. A little after that He cleared out."

Pence reached for the A&W. "All that's left of all that is Lily here. She'll just have to do for now. Trump thinks he's such a bad-ass, thought I should be so excited about hanging with him. What a laugh."

Shattering Mike Pence's nostalgic rage, John Boehner (pronounced BAYner) stumbled in with the latest issue of the Vatican News and Views. "Look at this," he yelled, wild-eyed. "Just look at it." He shook the paper in the face of Pence. Mike grew pensive.

"So what do you want me to do about it?" he growled. "Fatso's no longer my concern. He wants to sell 'Baby Trump' pills, I don't give a flying nun. I already got mine." He snatched a tiny replica as it lurched by and threw up. "Ain't it cute?"

"They're not for having a baby Trump. They're for preventing it."

"Oh, I see. He's gambling that the epidemic has been contained and nobody can say the pills didn't work. That will probably sell better than the other way. He is first and only a businessman."

"And what in the world are you doing with one?"

"Ah, just watching it for a friend. It's eerie seeing somebody you knew only as a man as a baby."

"Not much difference?"

"Yep. Just as delightful."

13

Suddenly "YOU'LL WONDER WHERE THE YELLOW WENT WHEN YOU BRUSH YOUR TEETH WITH PEPSODENT started showing up all over The Villages. Not actual signs but scrawled on benches, sidewalks, lamp posts. Star reporter Oldson suspected this a clue in the Beasley case. He just had to figure out what kind of a clue it was.

"What do you think, Maxine?" he plied his love while pouring hot cocoa for them both.

"About what, my love? There are so many screwy things going on, I can't catch up."

Jimmy's heart swelled with the innocence of his woman. "You know, the Pepsodent signs."

"Oh that. I just thought it might mean the end of the world was nigh or something like that."

"Maybe that's all it means. But if you think about it long enough, you'll wonder where the yellow went whether you brush your teeth with Pepsodent or not. 'You'll wonder where the yellow went.' Just think about that. Over and over. Will we wonder? Really? Or will it be too late? And actually, I never did know where the yellow went. But I never wondered about it either. Maybe we should wonder about where the yellow went. And other things too."

Maxine walked over and put her arm in Jimmy's. "I see what you mean. It could be a lie, something else for us to wonder about and be afraid of. If that really happened, we couldn't even see bananas."

"And there we would be, just like the prophecy, wondering where they went. I'm already hypothetically wondering... unless of course, nobody brushes their teeth with Pepsodent. That may be our only chance. We have to make sure we don't use Pepsodent and we won't have to worry about it."

"Or wonder where the yellow went..."

"Exactly. But we still wouldn't be able to see where the bananas are even if we don't wonder about it."

Maxine started bouncing around a little bit. "I know! 1 know! They paint the bananas."

Jimmy was about to place his freckled hand atop Maxine's when he heard footsteps near the front door. Nobody was there but as he looked around, his gaze fell on the door, upon which was scrawled in black magic marker the ubiquitous Pepsodent slogan.

"Maxine," he said quietly, "There's only one way to solve this mystery."

"What is that my love?' Maxine responded, taking his hand in hers. I wish to solve all mysteries...except the mystery of our love."

"We're going to have to brush our teeth with Pepsodent."

"I think I understand. We can't find out where the yellow went until we wonder about it."

"I love you Maxine."

"Oh my."

Before purchasing Pepsodent, Jimmy researched the enigmatic words and learned of their origin as a platitude Plato said to his followers in his early days, establishing him as an enigmatic man. Then he noticed scrawled on the back of a park bench in Lake Humpter Village: "Munch munch munch a bunch of Fritos... corn chips."

Jimmy retreated to the lee side of a street sign a block away and kept vigil, quickly rewarded by a shadowy figure approaching and obliterating with yellow paint the new slogan. At last with a breakthrough of sorts he apprehended the glacially escaping vandal.

He identified himself and said, "Why did you just do that?"

The slightly hunched priest looked at him bewildered and replied with moving but unspeaking lips. Then emerged the words "Ring around the collar."

The flabbergasted reporter pressed, "You did that because ring around the collar?"

He nodded.

"You have a ring around your collar?"

Again he appeared to struggle. "Away go trouble down the drain," he stated firmly and began walking away.

84

"What do you mean?"

"I mean," he said without turning around, "over and under, around and through, Pall Mall brings great flavor to you." He smiled in a bemused, grudging way and continued to his golf cart with the white flag.

The nonplussed reporter proceeded to Johnny Rocket's where he decisively ordered a bacon cheeseburger. "I deserve the bacon," he told himself. "And I don't have to be concerned with that level of economy anymore after the Enquirer piece. I'll just always have the bacon without even thinking about it."

The elderly waitress at the counter said, "Over under around and through, Johnny Rocket brings great flavor to you."

"What?!? that's what he just said. "What in the world is going on here?"

"Why, the world tastes better with Pall Mall," and she lit one between creased lips and handed it to him.

Gripped now with exploding fear, the star reporter stumbled backward through the door. "Maxine," he thought, "I must get to Maxine before it's too late."

Jimmy raced upstairs to his love nest and threw open the door. There sat his love on the small couch. She looked up adoringly, patted the cushion beside her, pulled open her shirt a smidgen and said, "Double your pleasure, double your fun."

"No, Maxine, no!" Jimmy wailed as he collapsed sobbing in her lap. Maxine patted his head, saying "No more tears...no more tears."

After a bit Jimmy sat up and asked Maxine what she would like to do for the remainder of the day. She rubbed Jimmy's leg and replied, "You deserve a break today."

"Maxine, my love, why are you speaking like this?" he implored.

"Well, my man," she explained, "they're always after my lucky charms."

Oldson lightly shook Maxine, like a caked up box of Shake 'n' Bake. He looked into her eyes. "Maxine. Are you in the there?"

"A little dab'll do ya," she replied sweetly.

Jimmy dropped her like a lead balloon and bolted toward the bathroom. There it was, by the sink. The one time used tube.

Out of the house the first time in three days, Barney Jenkins walked into Publix, snarling "What are you lookin' at?" to nobody in particular. Barney's favorite brand usually was whatever was on sale. It just so happened Pepsodent, cheap anyway, was Bogo. "Whadaya know?" he thought, "a BOGO matching need. I may live long enough to use these." Into the arm basket they went.

"I ain't been in here since they changed the deals on Thursday," Barney thought. "I wonder if Breyer's is on sale."

And there it was, buy one get one. First Barney's body chemistry moved in the far off direction of happy. Then he saw the price and it sprang back like a bungy chord. "Look at this," he shouted at an old crone trundling by in the wake of her cart. "The BOGO price is twice what the old regular price used to be. They hook you on mint chocolate chip and then jack it up."

"Well," she said, "It's the real thing."

"Sure but it just ain't right."

"Snap, crackle and pop," she said cheerfully and rolled down toward the popsickle section.

Even though Graham Crackers were never on sale, Barney splurged and bought a box of "originals," still wrapped in good old wax paper,' a special treat he allowed himself occasionally, to be doused in milk, real milk, not from wheat or oats but from an actual cow udder. To heck with Breyer's.

At checkout the young cashier asked him "Is plastic alright for you?"

"Used to be," Jenkins stabbed, "you gave me a choice. 'Paper or plastic?' you said. Now you're pushin' the plastic. One more choice I won't have for long, like American or National League. Well I say no. Plastic's not okay with me. I want to kill the rainforests, not the ocean. Gimme paper."

"I'm sorry. We don't have paper."

"What?!? You're just pretending to give me a choice? What madness is this? Democracy?"

The bag boy interjected, "You can buy a Publix bag and use it over and over again."

"So now the bagboy's piling on. Is this your routine? Well, guess what? I don't want any of it." Luckily for everyone, Barney was wearing an undershirt when he whipped off his shirt and said, "Put it all in there. That's what's alright for me."

Jimmy Oldson turned on his car radio, always tuned to The Villages a.m. station to hear if people were talking about the eerie speech defect. As *Tell Laura I Love Her* trailed off, DJ Needle Nabors said wistfully, "Well, he *had* go power."

Oldson ran back up the stairs, grabbed Maxine, threw her into his car and headed out of town to see if it was everywhere. He called the Daily Sun to tell Chief Editor Verry White what was going on. The crusty White told him, "You know, Jimmy, I'm stuck on Band Aids 'cause Band Aids are stuck on me." Oldson screamed.

Deep in the offices of the CIA, a place where forgotten people performed forgotten tasks for forgotten masters, a small light came on for the first time, a bulb almost as old as The Villages, installed shortly after the first phase of the subdivision had been completed. A cat yowled, the third cat trained specifically and only to yowl the moment that light came on. Then the cat died. Agent 31 walked over and read the instructions at the bottom of the cat's water bowl: If the cat has yowled, the Villagers are fouled: code name Illage Vidiots:

Agent 29a said, "What's that about, Phil?"

"Oh. It's just another one of those things from the past, finally come to fruition but we've already found it all out years ago. The cat food bill must have been enormous."

"That's like The Twilight Zone where the young guy goes to Mars and comes back old while his girlfriend stayed the same. All for nothin'."

"Yeah. The cat sure could have had a better life. Heck, I thought it was stuffed – haven't seen it move since I got here."

"Well, it's dead now."

"Yup."

In the Lady Lake Library Jimmy Oldson found what he was looking for in the microfilm file. He was horrified to learn that, in violation of truth, justice and the American way, from the 1950's through the 80's Baby Boomers were imprinted with slogans which became a permanent feature of their brain. "Under the burden of this and television shows particularly Leave it to Beaver, these brains never will be able to fully develop, just like Wally and the Beaver. To concentrate these people, we have built an irresistible replica of this time period to test if under these conditions the slogans will grow and gradually become the sole cognitive function of the inhabitants, thus producing a population of sustainable morons. When the time is right, the place will be bombarded by the Pepsodent slogan. If successful the light will come on triggering the cat."

14

Jimmy Oldson ensconced Maxine at the Holiday Inn in Ocala with strict orders to stay put while he shot back to the Villages to see how this all connected to Joe Beasley's demise. He decided to randomly ask people about it. The first three recited an eerily appropriate slogan, then he encountered Barney Jenkins who had grown up Mennonite and therefore never exposed to television or radio, not even knowing what they were until the age of thirty-three, about the same age as Daniel Boone when he kilt him a bar.

Oldson instantly recalled his previous meeting with Jenkins, slumped this time in his golf cart by the road gazing into the steering wheel. "Hello, sir," Oldson picked up the thread,

Jenkins jerked back into the world. "God Almighty, not you again. Another slow news day?"

"Hey, wait a minute," Oldson blurted, "why aren't you talking in slogans?"

Jenkins lowered his eyelids and viewed the reporter

askance. "You sure know how to kill a conversation, I'll give you that. Is that what you say to everybody? What slogan were you expecting?"

"Well," said the eager Oldson, "It wouldn't surprise me if you said, "You'll wonder where the yellow went.""

Maybe I'm just insane now, Jenkins thought. It's not so bad, really. Might even beat the alternative. "I thought you were still worried about what happened to Joe."

"I am but I'm having a hard time communicating out here."

That's not surprising, Jenkins thought. "Until I get the body exhumed for a real autopsy, we don't even know what got him, let alone who."

Just then Oldson vanished.

Well that does it, Jenkins thought. Think I'll just rip off my clothes and run around naked for a while.

Star reporter Jimmy Olsdson found himself in a very strange environment indeed, "What the ???" the only thought he had. Everything was very thick and without direction, variously and curiously colored bubbles seeming to be moving through. Then he heard what sounded like some sort of vocal sound. What appeared to be a large boulder rolled on by and there, beyond it was Agzorf ecstatic about the first successful attempt to bring a surface dweller into the ante-crust. The reporter in Jimmy was inspired to head that way and seek an interview.

"It's alive! It's still alive," Agzorf exclaimed through tears of joy. "Oh what have we here? Indeed. What have we here?"

Headway was not coming easily to Jimmy but already he had adapted to breathing the bubbles when he could catch up with them. Just then Gleeep came running up like a tail wagging golden retriever.

"Oh, Agzorf, look. It comes to us," Gleeep bloofed in their native tongue.

"All will be easy with these things," she agreed.

"I don't think we should eat this one."

"Certainly not. We must give it a mission."

"I am relieved about that," Gleeep said. "See how cute it is, and see how it comes to us, so trusting."

"Not trusting, just dumb. Trust must be built upon something. Stupid requires nothing."

As Jimmy approached, he noticed the lack of clothing upon Gleeep and Agzorf. Turning slightly away and shielding his eyes, he shouted, "Do you folks think you could put something on?" His voice sounded deeper, warped and slowed down.

"Put something on," Gleeep said in English. "What do you suppose he means by that?"

"We shall have to ask him."

Instead of continuing to look away, Oldson decided to admire the fine physique of Agzorf for journalistic reasons.

"What do you mean by 'put something on?' Is this not a preposition without an object?" Gleeep posed, pleased to show off his grasp of surface talk.

Agzorf approached Oldson and felt of his garments. "Is this a part of you?"

Oldson said, "This is ridiculous. Where is this and

how did I get here?"

Because Gleeep knew nothing of deceit, he replied, "We have developed a machine that brought you here. Eventually we will bring more from what you call The Villages and we will eat them. We will bring the ones that look like your great fatman. We are very excited about this."

"Okay but where is this?

"Our civilization thrives directly below yours."

"Golly. What a story."

"We will send you back now. Tell the fatones to prepare. They now have a purpose in life"

"Wait a second. I have some things to ask you."

"Never mind. Only tell them to eat well and often. And to prepare to be enjoyed."

Jimmy popped back in time to see Barney Jenkins sitting on the rear seat of his golfcart pulling off his pants to reveal ceramic-white hairless legs receiving apparently first contact with sunlight. Jenkins lunged with one pants leg still hanging on, tackling the intrepid reporter around the waist and bringing him down.

"This is very important to me," Barney gasped, lying 95% nude on top of the struggling reporter "where you just went and how. The rest of my life depends on it."

"Good thing these cell phones are cameras too," Bud Tinsley chortled as he snapped a few shots from different angles. I don't know what in the world you're doing Barney, but I think I've heard of it. I'm sure glad I was walking by for this demonstration. Gotcha! And your cable tv too."

"Shit," Jenkins muttered as he listened to Tinsley's whooping fade in the distance.

Jimmy Oldson's muffled voice was fighting its way out of his mouth flattened against the concrete walkway and out from under Barney Jenkins' globular self. "Please get off me, mister."

"Not 'til you tell me what just happened or Hell freezes over." Jenkins tried to press down even harder than gravity provided.

"You have to put your pants back on."

"Alright but you better make it worth my while."

Barney rolled over and Oldson sprang out like a jack-in -the - box, thought about running but the reporter in him stopped his legs and he remained a safe distance away.

As Barney started reinstating his pants, Buz Murdock strolled by. "That's not cool, man."

"And what's cool?" Jenkins retorted. "You? Just going around through life with your pants on deciding for everybody else what's cool and what's not?!? I say it is cool. And you want to see what's even more cool?"

Murdock panicked. "No, no man. It's all cool. You're makin' the scene like an iceberg. It's cool, man. Cool. I'm just out here checking things out, didn't think I'd see anything this cool. I'll back you up Daddio, I'll fight for your right to be this cool."

"Yeah sure. Buz off." Barney put his other leg in and pulled his pants up.

"The first thing I want to know," Oldson said, "is why

you were out here naked when I got back."

"Hey. If you're talkin' to somebody and they just disappear, wouldn't you take your clothes off?"

Jimmy brightened. "Well yeah, I guess so."

"Alright. I'm glad we got that settled. If I keep my pants on this time is gonna have a lot to do with what you say next . Now how did you do that?"

"First let me ask you this: You were looking at me and then I just disappeared? Like instantly? Or did I kind of dissolve?"

Jenkins' hands went toward the zipper.

"Don't do that," the frightened reporter warned. "I need your help on this. I don't know what happened. It was like some weird dream. You're sure I didn't just fall asleep?"

The zipper started descending.

"Alright, alright."

Oldson described where he went and told of the naked people there, leaving out some details like their location and their message.

"So that's all you got."

The reporter nodded sincerely.

"How do you think this ties in with Joe gettin' killed?"

"Lots of strange things going on here, that's for sure Mr. ...."

"Mister'll do."

"But you really did see me disappear."

"And reappear."

So something must have happened to me, Jimmy thought, heading for his car. What if that was all true, about eating the fat Villageers? I have to call Mr. White, see if he can talk yet. We may have to go straight to Lantana with this one.

Jimmy barged into the office of Verry White to find him leaning back in his editor chair snipping with scissors at a piece of folded paper. On seeing Oldson, White exuberantly urged the cub reporter to watch as he opened the paper out to view the amazing designs he had created.

Oldson grabbed him by the shoulders and shook him, yelling, "Chief! Chief! Snap out of it."

White viewed him quizzically and said with a sense of wonder, "I can't believe I ate the whole thing."

Jimmy shook him some more. "Chief! Chief! The CIA did this to you." White just sat there and giggled. Suddenly a large man with an S printed on his shirt, and his underpants visible over his tights busted through the wall and said, "Allow me." Oldson stepped back and the stranger shook the editor back to normal. Before Jimmy could thank him he was gone.

"Who was that man?" White asked.

"I don't know, S Man? He's got go power, that's for sure."

Verry White added, "There he goes."

Oldson continued, "He's eating his Cheerios!"

White put his hand over his mouth, then he and the cub reporter had a much needed, if uneasy laugh.

It was reported that the men with S's on their shirt went

all over the Villages shaking people back to normal. Finding it redundant, the CIA pulled the plug on the program anyway so The Great Slogan Time, as it would come to be known, gradually dissipated.

15

Mike Pence sat down next to Barney Jenkins on the back of his golf cart, slightly compressing the springs. Barney looked at the extremely pale man without surprise. "Look, I just want you to know I'm not Mike Pence," Pence said.

"I want you to know I am Mike Pence," Barney said.

"That will work. I want you to spread the word."

"What word?"

"That's not Mike Pence."

"That's two words and a jerk."

Pence sighed, "You look like a man who can handle it."

"What's in it for me?"

"You get to assist a great American."

"Who?"

"Alfred Hitchcock."

Jenkins shifted to make space between him and Pence. "Humh. Are you a homo?"

Mike Pence considered the question. "Yes, yes I am. I'm a homo erectus and Mike Pence is not. You can remember it that way. And prove it to others. You see, Mike Pence is in Washington."

"Okay. And where does Alfred Hitchcock fit into all this?"

"You've heard of the famous gunslinger Wild Bill Hitchcock, haven't you? Well, that's where."

"Okay," Jenkins said, "I'll do it. Now get off my cart before I call a cop."

Donald Trump farted in a box and mailed it to Senate Majority Leader Mitch McConnell. "Another empty box from Trump," one of his aides said.

"Yeah. I wonder what it means."

John Smith hadn't been out the house since his disgrace at second base, and hadn't seen the Pepsodent slogans. He fondled his colostomy bag, vaguely surprised that, though he could feel it, it could not feel him. As he racked his brain for a four letter word meaning contents ending in "t", Pocahontas entered with his afternoon glass of Bosco. "You deserve a break today. Why don't you stick with the Mayberry crosswords?"

"Heck, Goober could do those. I need a challenge since I'm banned from sports."

"What about your special Sport Bag? That doesn't put a tiger in their tank?"

"Nah. Said they don't want to have to inspect everybody for Sport bags."

99

"You could try harder in a bag league."

"Even if they do start one up, it wouldn't be the same. The challenge was to get away with playing in the normal leagues. Anyway I don't want to play in a bag league. There'd be no coming back from that. Pretty soon I'm defined by my colostomy. Probably have to give it a name like it's a parasite."

"Is it a man?"

"I don't know."

"Make it English and you can call it Colin."

"That's just great. People pass me on the street and say, "Hi, John. How's Colin?""

"To be polite they might say Hi to Colin and ask him about you."

Yeah, it would never end. Probably have to play bag Scrabble, stand in the colostomy bag line at Publix, listen to WBAG, subscribe to COLOSTOMY..."

"You could be a real bag boy."

"Sure. I could say, 'Plastic, paper or colostomy?'"

"You'd be a hit, you two. And it would get you out of the house."

"Yeah, I'm real excited about it. And all because of that one time on second base."

"Well, how about if you got your butt reconnected? That shouldn't be so hard to do. Away go troubles down the drain."

John sighed and shrugged his shoulders. "Don't you think they'd have done that in the first place? The whole point was to disconnect my butt."

"What does your butt even do anymore?"

"Nothin'. I can't even fart."

"Weird. Did they sew it up?"

"Alright, that's enough. Suppose we could talk about something else now?"

"You know, if everybody got reconnected, that would Make America Fart Again. Methane is a greenhouse gas so that would speed up global warming. You're helping save the planet, John."

"Great."

"You know, there's rumors about having a colostomy bag loofah. Does she or doesn't she?"

John looked up from his puzzle. "Yeah?"

"Yes. There was an unfortunate incident at the Blownwood Cinema with Margaret Truman of all people. In sight it's not always right."

"Well why not? Why shouldn't she have one? What's wrong with anybody having a colostomy bag?"

"Oh, nothing, dear. It's miles better than having the colostomy without the bag. Just imagine that. I wouldn't be able to take you anywhere. I wonder if they had the operation before they invented the bag. People just kind of laying across the toilet when they had to go."

John Smith looked up again from the puzzle. "You sure are one for looking at every side of a thing. I always liked that about you, makes a person think. I'll bet they would have had special stand-up toilets. Or they could just hold a bowl out there."

"The bag way is better."

"Oh, I agree. They ought to have decoy bags and make it a Villages rule that everyone has to wear one, like WW2 when Germans all acted like Jews so you couldn't tell the difference. That way I can stop being discriminated against."

"That was people in Denmark that did that."

"Oh. But we can still do it here."

Pocahontas said, "I'm going to start right now with a letter to the editor."

"Alright but make it anonymous."

"You bet. I don't want people thinking I have one...not that there's anything wrong with that. You know, Margaret's the one who found Joe Beasley, the Quicker Picker-Upper."

"Hmm. What if she killed Joe because he knew about her bag?"

"It's been done for less."

At the Lady Lake Republikins fer a Better Trump headquarters Klansman Curtis Baumgardner was not trusting his ears and more than a little skeptical of the source of the sound. "So you're tellin' me, Wayne, that this reporter from the newspepper come in here and sez how he'd like to come to our lynchin' if'n we'd be so good as to have one. Been a while. Is that right?"

"Let a dog piss on yer mother's grave if it ain't."

"No Wayne, it's let a dog piss on *your* mother's grave. You're the one sayin' it."

"My maw ain't even dead yet."

"Well when she is, let a whole pack o' dogs do everthing on her grave if'n you're makin' this up. Actually, fer now they kin piss on her."

"You take that back."

"Sure Wayne, I'll take it back. Let a nigger piss on her."

"That did it." Clueless advanced on Baumgardner.

"Alright, alright, no need gettin' excited about it. I'll take it back. About the nigger."

"Thet's good Curtis 'cause I might jest put a big sign with a arrow out where your maw's buried sayin' NIGGERS PISS HEAR. How'd you like that? There'd be a hunnerd niggers ever day pissin' on yer maw."

"Shoot. They ain't a hunnerd niggers around there what kin read."

"They only need one."

Just then Jimmy Oldson popped back in to check on the date of the luncheon.

"Hi. I'm Jimmy Oldson with the Daily Pla... er, Village Sun. Did you get a better Trump yet?" he said with jocularity.

"This is the feller right here, Curtis. Walter Conkrite. You go ahead and ast him."

Curtis hitched up his red nylon pants with his bony little hands. "Fergit about Trump fer now. I herd your excited about us puttin' on a lynchin' sometime."

"Sure. Then I can do a story on your organization and what you plan to do for the community."

"Lynchin' don't bother you none?"

"Golly no. I'm almost always hungry."

This shocked even Curtis. "We wasn't talkin' 'bout roastin' 'im. What kinda people are you over here?"

Wayne said, "I told ya Curtis. Looks like nothin's pissin' on my mama's grave."

"Nope. She's safe fer now. But Wayne," Curtis whispered in his ear, "who'd wanta eat a nigger? Jest thinkin' 'bout it makes me sick."

"Mebbe thet's how they does it these days. We been fallin' behin' the times."

"Thing iz," Curtis confided to Jimmy, "I see why you ain't had none in a long time, 'cause they just flat ain't anybody here to lynch. The only jig I seen was drivin' a U.S mail truck and he was in and out right quick, like he knowed you folks was on the lookout fer one."

Baumgardner re-hitched up his pants. "So thet's gonna be a problem. We could go out somewheres and ketch one and fetch it here but local's better. Looks kinda weird, people be sayin' why you dragging him over here? Whynchew lynch him back where he done his evil deeds?"

Unable to fathom anything he was hearing, Oldson was starting to wonder if this was an organization composed entirely of mental incompetents. Or maybe that's some kind of MAGA humor.

"What do you have to catch? A turkey for the luncheon? Is that a tradition with your group? Have to catch everything you eat?"

"Now he's talking code," Curtis whispered to Wayne. "You know what the turkey is, right?"

104

"I knows alright," said Wayne and winked. "And I bet he likes the dark meat."

Baumgardner was furious. "Don't you never wink at me again, Wayne. You unnerstand?"

Baumgardner composed hisself and faced the reporter. "I don't go in for none of that winkin."

Just then the black mailman appeared.

"Well, lookie what we got here," Wayne Clueless said.

The postman looked around and said, "I damn sure want a better Trump."

"Why do you want a better Trump? You hate Trump. You don't want any kind of a Trump."

"Are you kidding? I'm all for him. But he could always be improved."

"Why is you for him?" Clueless asked.

"Well to tell the truth, in spite of this dark exterior, I've always been white as you on the inside. Maybe whiter. One day I was sitting there watching that sweet Aunt Bea bustling around taking care of Andy and Opy and suddenly I realized why I didn't fit in with my family and everybody. I was really white. You can't imagine how liberating that was."

Nobody said anything for half a minute. "Let me ask you this," Curtis Baumgardner finally posed, "If'n you wuz going to lynch somebody, would you ruther lynch a white man or a black un?"

"Oh, black all the way, my man. White folks aren't for lynching. I get the feeling I could get right into it with the proper provocation."

"Well there you have it, Wayne, I guess 'bout ennything kin happen these days. This here is one of them biologic freaks ... like a albino catfish."

"Well boy," Curtis said turning to the postman, "yer the best nigger I ever seen, no denyin' it, and I don't expeck to see a better one. But you kin act as white as Wonderbread, wear a post office shirt, kiss Donald Trump's ass if you need to, vote for 'im three times but the fact is, you're still jest a nigger. And a dumb one at that."

Clueless got excited. "Whaddaya say we lynch *him*, Curtis?"

"We already been over that, Wayne."

"Yeah but this is diff'rent. Spose we say if he lets us lynch him, thet would prove he's white."

Baumgardner looked with new respeck upon Wayne. "You know, Wayne, thet's the closest I ever heared you come to havin' a good idea."

Wayne blushed and looked at his loafers. "Thanks, Curtis."

"But I still don't think she'll fly. Mr. Postman, let me ax you this. If we wuz to have a lynchin', I's just supposin' now, just talkin' here, how'd you feel 'bout bein' the guest of honor? What I'm suggestin' here is, if you wuz to deliver yourself, which like I jus' said, is a nigger, for the festivities, then thet would prove you's white."

Jimmy Oldson couldn't help butting in at that point. "That doesn't make any sense, Mr. ..."

"Baumgardner."

"Mr. Baumgardner. He can't be white and a nigger. I

106

mean, a colored person. Sorry."

"That's okay. Lots of folks think that but it doesn't come out." He turned to Baumgardner. "I think I'll respectfully turn down your invitation, my fellow white man, because I don't require your validation. I already know I'm white and I'd rather stay alive and enjoy my tv shows. Might even move into The Villages someday."

"See, Wayne? There ain't no gettin' around 'em these days."

Cub reporter Oldson asked, "Sir, are you married?"

"I'm pleased to say I am."

"Is your wife also 'white?"

"Yes he is."

Curtis staggered backwards and grabbed hold of a chair. "What'd you say? Your wife's a he?"

"Is he ever." The postman beamed. "We got married last year."

"Baumgardner looked to Wayne for something familiar to fix on. "What we got here Wayne, is a queer nigger thinks he's white and thet he's married to a white man. And he's deliv'rin' the Nunited States Mail! I want to string it up so bad. On'y thing is we can't be lynchin' the mailman."

"Curtis, that makes me madder than if he was with a white woman. It jus' makes my skin crawl."

"It's the transniggeration of America, Wayne. We're seein' it with our own two eyes."

"We take his post office shirt before we lynch 'im, there's nobody'd know what his job was."

"Nah, we'd get the feds on us sure. We migh's well

107

just go to the moon, Wayne. We gots nothin' more to do aroun' here."

The postman dropped off an AARP recruitment flier, encouraged everyone to Make America Gay Again and continued on his rounds whistling the Donna Reed Show theme song.

Oldson had all he cared for of trying to keep up with the banter. "So do you know when this luncheon's going to be?"

Curtis and Wayne exchanged looks of infinite exasperation. "Where wuz you the las' ten minnits? Affagavistan? Ain't a gonna be no lynchin."

16

With Villageers slowly reverting to normal, if inane speech, Jimmy Oldson refocused on trying to break the Beasley case wide open.

Verry White was leaning back, cigar dangling and feet on desk. "Oldson, did you know, a lake without turtles is like a lake with turtles?"

"Well, no, Mr. White, I don't think I ..."

... "Unless you wish to see turtles."

"Wow, Chief. I never thought of it like that."

"Don't call me Chief!" White retracted his legs and sat up. "Look, son, I know you think Beasley's demise was connected to these subterranean people you think you discovered, but people die all the time in The Villages. It's one of the most popular causes of death. They're all walking around with expiration dates like a package of pork chops. Some go before they go off, some after. Some way after. From what you say about Beasley, he probably did his time well and got early release."

"Okay but what about the plot to suck everybody down

there for food? Shouldn't we warn people?"

"Do we know of any way to defend against it?"

"No."

"Well then, alerting people to danger without offering a way to avoid it would only cause needless panic."

"I see what you mean."

"Why don't we just drill a hole and pull these hungry subterraneans out? Set 'em up with food stamps."

"Wouldn't *that* be a story, Mr. White."

"I'll tell you what, Jimmy. Before we start handing out shovels, we'll have some kind of a sonogram done of the area, see if anything weird shows up."

"Gee, Mr. White. That'll be great!"

"In the meantime get down there and cover the opening of registration for The Villages high school."

"You got it Chief. Maybe I'll go get Maxine and see if she's interested in signing up."

"You just do that. Might be a good angle on the story: Sixty year old virgin gives birth to Donald Trump and starts high school. But you can't enlist. You're too young. And don't call me Chief!"

"Yeah, hey. I better give her my ring so she doesn't start dating some one else."

"Go for it, kid."

Oldson liberated his love from motel guest arrest and brought her down to the big registration tent at the site of the new school, Orson Wells High, As they drove there, Oldson poked the baby. "How's the little Trumpster?" he

110

asked,

"He's not 'the little Trumpster.' He's our baby and don't you forget it."

"You sure it's the same one?"

Maxine's face flushed with fury.

"Alright, Maxine, I'm sorry. That's the first time I've ever seen you angry."

"How dare you suggest that this isn't our wonderful baby? Anyway I don't care about all those other ones. And besides, ours is getting cuter all the time."

"He sure is," Jimmy responded "I think he's the cutest one."

"That's more like it."

"... but, you know, it's all your cuteness. I had nothing to do with it."

"How can you say that, Jimmy? You were right there with me through it all. Talking about what we'd name it, how miraculous it was that we got to have a baby together."

"You know we still haven't named it."

"Yes, I know, but...are you trying to get out of your responsibilities young man!?!"

"Maxine, sweetheart, I've never seen you like this. It kind of turns me on."

"Oh, Jimmy. That's what Joe never said to me. Let's skip school."

Ten minutes later Jimmy preceded Maxine out of the car, filled the stroller with the baby and headed once more toward the high school, Oldson reminding her that he had to get back on the Beaslley case right after this.

The principal, Miss Brooks, was there to greet everybody: "Now remember. This is high school. Not everybody gets to do it over. Don't squander the opportunity. All those things you've been wishing you had done differently, better grades, better boyfriend, be openly gay, explode a cherry bomb in the toilet, here's your chance to do just that. Luckily they don't sell cherry bombs anymore. Due to insurance considerations we can't have a football team from the student body but we'll hire two teams to play each other Friday night the year 'round, one of them representing The Villages. We'll be seating you in the classrooms by age so you'll all be sophomores, juniors or seniors. Don't tell anyone you heard it from me, but you seniors might want to think about flunking so you can repeat next year."

Miss Brooks hailed Buz Murdock. "Mr. Buz Murdock will be your guidance counselor. I think we all know that Mr. Murdock's moral standards are of the highest order, perhaps even higher. Rely on Buz to guide you through the challenges of high school as no guidance counselor has ever done."

To a smattering of applause, mostly from Miss Brooks, Murdock took the microphone. "Let me tell you this right now straight from my main area of expertise. This is not cool. But it's all you got. So let's do it right!" The crowd cheered. Jerry Mathers had a heart attack and died.

"People are trying to say that was the Beaver that died out there. No way. That wasn't the Beav. No way," Ward Cleaver posted on Facebook from his cyrogenic chamber."

The next day the local MAGA group held a protest march with signs like NO DEAD BEAVERS in the VILLAGES, BEAVER is ALIVE, YOU CANT KILL BEAVER and BE A BEAVER BELIEVER. Lumpy said, "The little puke was all excited. Thought he was finally going to be a big kid. Now you'll never be a big kid, Beaver."

Wally said, "Shut up, Lumpy. What'd he have to go and have a stupid heart attack for?"

The obit in the Village Sun was short:

"Jerry Mathers, better known as Beaver Cleaver although never caught in the act, tipped over while finally registering for high school. His much cooler brother, who got to go to high school, beat up Lumpy at the funeral. Local woke activist Curtis Baumgardner said, "Thet show was stupid anyway. Everbody wuz white. What's the good in bein white if'n there ain't no niggers?" Fellow activist Wayne Clueless went further. "Shoot. Ain't no fun bein' *alive* without niggers." Mathers' friend Whitey, representing the Villages said, "I was frozen in time with Beaver. And he was such a dork. This will give me a chance to move on." Whitey was hung in effigy from a live oak at Lake Humpter Square as a series of protests against Mathers' death was being planned.

Mathers had no descendants and precious few ancestors."

Protestors felt somehow a little wrong about hanging the sign on Whitey identifying the effigy; but their zeal carried them through. After the crowd had thinned, two men stood beneath the dangling representation. "Will you look at that?" Curtis Baumgardner said to Buddy Burnsed, wiping a tear from his eye, "These folks is lynchin' dolls jest to stay in practice."

"Doll's the wrong color, Curtis."

"They jest don't want to be too obvious about it. But we kin fix that."

Next morning a crowd had gathered around the suspended doll, silent with wonder as they gazed up at the transfigured victim.

Finally Betty Blooper started tearing her clothes and screaming repeatedly, "It's a miracle."

Preacher Roe, from the Church of Almost Everybody's Already Dead arrived on the scene. Standing under it, he proclaimed, "This is not the work of God. This is the work of the devil."

But he was shouted down then by the crowd, content in their vindication by The Almighty. From as far away as Ontario, gawkers began arriving in The Villages to witness the phenomenon.

"Another one for the Enquirer, Mr White?"

"God turns white doll black? I don't think so, Jimmy. I say we cut that thing down and run some tests. This is no miracle, unless God is relying on spray paint these days."

"He might, sir, now that the flourocarbons are out of it."

"It's getting pretty hard to keep up with all the supernatural stuff around here. How about your mole people? Can we connect them to this? Kind of tidy things up a little?"

Oldson brightened. "That way, we could kill two birds with one stone."

"It would certainly be nice. That's the problem. Too many birds flying around, not enough stones."

Thousands of northerners a day were funneling down 441 to witness the miracle, and an armed guard had been placed to ensure sanctity. American Africans across the country waited for the next foot to drop,

Asked about it, Donald Trump shrugged. "I don't know. But if God did that, well, God knows what he's doing, right? A Hell of a leader. What's God saying? Everybody should be black? It's hard to tell. It really is. Maybe God thought that was a pretty funny thing to do. We'll just have to wait and see. It may take a long time. A very, very long time. The longest time you can have. Who knows? Who really does? Nobody does know. Nobody. We'll find out one day. Maybe if all white people start staying white again. And dolls. Lots of dolls. Then we'll know something."

Meanwhile at Seismology R Us in Lady Lake, Ed Asner was putting his phone down. "Hey Pete."

"Yeah, what?"

"Just had an odd call from Verry White, editor of a great metropolitan newspaper in The Villages."

"Yeah? Does he want another earthquake prediction for Sumter County? Maybe a tsunami warning?"

"Nah. Weirder. Wants us to take radar readings all over The Villages. Doesn't know what he's looking for, just wants us to report anything we can't explain."

"Hell, I got plenty of that already. I can't explain why I'm still livin' in Lady Lake doing goofy crap like this. I can't explain why I ain't rich yet workin' for you. I can't ex..."

"I get the point. Your life is one giant mystery. But let's humor this nut. He's what they call a "paying customer.""

"Jimmy, I'm not going to relive high school. There's only one thing I would have changed and you already took care of that."

The object of Maxine Falderall's speech swelled with pride. "Besides I want to devote all the time I can to being a mommy." With this declaration Jimmy nearly exploded with devotion.

After calming down a little, Oldson asked, "Has he called you Mama yet?"

"Well no, I can't tell exactly what he's trying to say. It sort of sounds like Toots. At that moment their baby distinctly yelled from its bassinet, "Hey Tits!"

"Maxine, I don't think he's going to make it to Mama. It just called you Tits."

"Oh my, where did he learn to talk like that?"

"I don't know but he knows what he wants. I guess you better go give it to him. Anyway, I have an interview with Margaret Truman in a half hour."

"Ooh. Is she a suspect?"

"She has one thing going for her. She's the last person anyone would suspect. You can't imagine her slowing down long enough to kill anybody."

"Maybe she ran him over."

"Wouldn't that be something. I just have to get her to admit it."

"Hit and run. Nobody wants to admit to that."

"Yeah but this would be run and hit. You never know. She might slip up."

"I think you should wring it out of her."

"Maxine!"

"I did care for Joe, you know, a long time ago."

"Nice to meet you Mr. Oldson," Margaret opined from her Stairmaster. "Come on in and tell me what you want out of this interview."

"First I want to tell you that you're an inspiration to all the Villageers, with all your get up and go."

"You mean I've got Go Power? Cheerios aren't my secret," she said while upping her speed.

"What is your secret?"

"It's a fact that if I keep going all the time, my teeth won't decay. They can't decay if you're always moving or doing something. I just hope to die before I have to go to the dentist again."

"Wow. This is great. So it's a race between death and the dentist."

"Slowest one wins, like these bicycle races where it's

117

the last one over the finish line."

"When did you embark on this form of oral hygiene, Miss Truman?"

"Call me Ms."

"Sorry, Ms. Truman."

"Ten years ago. I saw it on an internet site that was quickly shut down by the government because it told the truth."

"And you haven't had a cavity since then?"

"Certainly not. I've got false teeth, see?"

Oldson was stunned as the top teeth emerged on the end of her tongue. "But if you have false teeth, you don't need to keep moving."

"Just thought I'd err on the side of caution. Got the idea watching *Fail Safe*. When I saw how foolproof the government can make something and it still goes wrong, well I knew I should never get complacent."

"When did you get the false teeth?"

'Twelve years ago."

"That wasn't foolproof enough for you?"

"Suppose my teeth started growing back?"

"Well you sure covered all your bases."

"Do you think this story might start a craze?"

"Sure."

She slowed her pace. "I could be the next Jane Fonda."

"I think you already are, Ms. Truman. One last thing. Have you ever bumped into anybody while running, you

118

know, hurt somebody?"

"Knocked Hell out of Mike Pence one day, or anyway some guy who looked just like him. Just walking along talking to himself, not looking where he was going.

"He was kind of raving. He said something real weird to me. He said God told him He was going to try to avert the rapture, He said how we shouldn't be fooled, that He wasn't the one organizing that, it was some guys from another planet that are going to hover overhead and just suck everybody up like a giant Hoover. It didn't happen yet because they're still ironing the kinks out....yeah and he said God said they tried it on the moon and it worked fine, got all the moonmen but Earth is a lot bigger, got trees and buildings getting in the way."

"Hmm. Did you see him real good?"

"Broad daylight. Say, what is this? You think I knocked over Joe? You think *I* killed him?"

"No, I didn't say that."

"Is Pence dead?"

"I don't think so."

"Okay I lied to you. I've had one cavity all that time. And I didn't see any dentist to fill it, if you know what I mean. If somebody killed Joe, I sincerely hope you find out who. But you can stop wasting your time with me. I lacked motive"

"We'll still do the story on your dental program."

17

B ack at Seismology R Us, Ed Asner was toying with ways to simulate earthquakes when Pete came in from the first radaring of The Villages underground.

"Hi, Pete. I'm just thinking if we could make people think the ground is shaking, we'd get a lot more business."

"You promise not to do that and you might squeeze out a nice subsidy from some real estate companies. Or... we could just relocate to someplace where there are actually faults."

"Oh, this place has plenty of those."

"Yeah but they're not making us any money."

Asner perched on the corner of his desk, hands in his lap. "Money, money, money. Is that all you can think about?"

"Nope. I think about those days we're downwind of The Villages and it's like living in a giant fart. They should put out alerts."

"That's why we got Old Glory out there."

"But sometimes it comes in at night when we're sleeping and we wake up in it."

"That's the stench of money Pete. That's why we're here. Got this whole God-forsaken territory to ourselves. We just have to market our services better."

If all you care about is having no competition, why didn't you go to The Arctic and sell flip flops? There's a wide open field for you."

"Speaking of business, how'd your sonogram go? Is the ground pregnant?"

"Yeah, we're gonna have little Teddy Roosevelts poppin' up everywhere."

"You know, we should run a special: get your yard sonogrammed. See what you own all the way down to Hell. Get 'em a framed picture."

"Now you're talkin', Pete. We just need to get creative."

Pete became thoughtful. "Why do you suppose anybody'd want to live there, with nobody young around?"

"I figure they just don't want to see what they aren't anymore. Don't want some punk calling 'em Pops."

"We oughtta fight back with a place old people can't live. Call it …"

"Neverland."

"Perfect. And have it just like The Villages with all the old timey stuff, but only young people living there. That would frost these old crabs, wouldn't it? And like here, where your grandkids can't visit you more than a week, in Neverland, your grandparents can't stay."

"And they couldn't show any new movies. Have to be all *Casablanca* and stuff."

"*The Blob*."

"Yeah. All the greats. Shit. I'd move in there."

"No way Jose. You're too old. I'm havin' it nobody over twenty-five."

"You'd be there about six months."

"Naw, I'll be grandfathered in."

"Yeah. So how'd the sonograms come out?"

"Bout what you'd expect. I wonder what they're angling for."

"Maybe people want to have basements or something."

"Water table's too high. Who knows? There were some anomalies down there."

"Maybe you found Capone's vault."

"His toilet'd be more our luck."

"Well we just collect the data and hand it over to the customer. They want interpretation," Ed said jingling two quarters in his pocket, "that's extra."

In the Earth's crust, Agzorf was disturbed. 'What the Hell was that?" she bloofed.

"Got me," Gleeep bloofed back. "It's like I got touched."

"You think they figured out we're here?"

"Wouldn't take a genius after you told that one we caught where we are and what we're going to do. Maybe they don't agree with your plan."

"How could that be? It benefits them also, so crowded

up there. We relieve them of all that cholesterol and fat that's getting in their way."

"Don't forget you created all those fatnesses."

"I didn't create it. I can't create anything. I just put the available fat in uniform packages."

"Will the tops be full of fat also?"

"Yes.. They will all be made just as they are now. The heads promise to be quite a delicacy. Perhaps we can enjoy them as they do their coconuts, with a straw through an eye hole."

"Agzorf, perhaps we should advance the timeline."

"Hmm...perhaps."

"And maybe when they ripen we should take them as we need them, instead of all at once."

"That could be a very efficient idea. Why should we preserve them here? They might not even notice if we take only a few at a time."

"That might ensure a continuing resource instead of a one time thing."

"Gleeep, I think you're very smart."

18

The first day of school saw not only a whole lot of fartin' goin' on but a whole lot of flirtin'. And sometimes simultaneously, almost like a Villages mating call. The rule most implemented and creatively violated was the prohibition of students of opposite sex foraying to the bathroom simultaneously. Regarding this, an addendum was added to prohibit cell phones and walkie talkies, students eventually frisked at the entrance. Still, inter-classroom bathroom visits could be prearranged with no way to prevent them.

To inhibit abuse of the restroom facilities, cameras were mounted out of reach in the ceiling. This feature, however proved for many less deterrent than incentive. Buz Murdock had his hands full. He thought about a return to paddling but concluded that might also encourage offenders.

Armed with a prepared speech, the guidance counselor addressed the student body over the intercom, the Route 66 theme music droning in the background. "Okay, you

Villageers, I'm a little disappointed in your behavior. This is school. In order to make school scool, you have to kick the "H" out of it and "H" doesn't stand for "swell." You're here to learn, remember? All the things you didn't learn first time around. As of today the student std rate is 33% higher than the Villages average, which, as we all know is number 1 in the nation. I know many of you take a certain hometown pride in that distinction but if it continues to rise, we could be shut down by the Sumter County Health Department. Maybe you can get vd from a toilet seat. But I doubt it. Me, what do I care what you do in the bathrooms? Anything you do in there, even what you're supposed to do, is going to be disgusting. A bathroom is a disgusting place. That's why they're always out of sight. But it doesn't have to be degrading. Whatever it is you do there, do it with caution or we'll have an epidemic on our hands. That makes me look bad. This is my first real job so whaddaya say you do it for me. Let's get a Buz on."

Spit wads pelted intercom speakers in every classroom. Condom dispensers were installed in the restrooms.

With football season coming up, Miss Brooks made an important announcement. "Ladies, here is a chance to recapture the glory and those without past glory to have it now and mingle with the crowd that never was your crowd. Cheer-leading tryouts are now open."

The Villages Woman's Club volunteered to organize the group and Pocahontas Smith, once leading cheer for the Seattle Savages, provided the expertise. Everybody made the squad who tried out with any zeal at all, including centenarian Emily Barnhorst.

Miss Brooks committed the oversight of not requiring underwear, so the male sports fans devoted most of their spectating to trying to get a glimpse of something. Those female spectators with underpants took the cue and removed them, giggling, in the restroom. Play was suspended midway through the second quarter as nobody was watching anymore, over, under, around and through, the bleachers having descended into a free-for-all. The cheerleaders headed for the players.

Later people would recall Barnhorst's vivid proclamation, "Damned if I'll be the only one with underwear on."

Mike Pence crawled out naked and pale as a waterlogged earthworm from under a pile of wriggling flesh under the bleachers, grabbed somebody's pants and staggered out of the melee, feeling satisfied for the first time in quite a while. He almost felt like God was with him again.

Meanwhile Joe Beasley's spirit, severed from his body in the failed first attempt by Agzorf to capture a surface dweller, was feeling extremely frustrated, confronted, as it were, by inability to utilize the astonishingly great body of Agzorf. It turns out, after you're just a spirit, it feels like you still have all your appendages in working order; but like any phantom limb, impossible to find.

While this fun football game was happening directly above him, Joe Beasley still was not satisfied with the explanation given him for his new location and condition.

"God dammit, did my whole body get amputated?"

126

"Is that what you think?" Gleeep asked, trying to be cagey.

"What do you mean 'Is that what I think?' What the Hell am I supposed to think?"

"As near as we can tell you," Agzorf said, "We think you're dead as a blandix. Somehow we got your consciousness and unfortunately your voice but the body, the only part we want, remained behind."

"Well can you get it please? I'd like to put it back on while I still can. I was doing alright, you know, finally, and then you assholes had to pull this shit."

"We are not assholes," Gleeep said in his wife's defense. "You are an asshole."

"I'm an asshole? That's rich. Did I kill you? Shit. I can't believe this is happening."

"Gleeep," Agzorf said, "Is it possible? He's no good to us or anybody like this."

"We don't know where his body is anymore."

"Thanks to you it's in the goddamm cemetery you idiots."

"Yes of course – where all your people are packaged. We can see what we can do."

"Well, I'm in pretty damn bad shape by now. Do you mind getting on it? I was supposed to get embalmed so I should at least look alright. I don't know what you're going to do for guts."

"We can try focusing on your words and put the beam in reverse, see what happens."

"Well that's just great. We'll see what happens. Just

get on with it. I can't wait to find out."

Gleeep pulled the lever and then called out, "Mr. Beasely. Mr. Beasley." There was no response. He looked at Agzorf and shrugged his shoulders. "Well, back to the drawing board." Rumors of a zombie lurching around The Villagers after dark largely were dismissed, many of the residents too closely resembling the description.

Joe Beasley is disillusioned with The Villages life after death. "Shit. I'm back but I can't do anything anyway. Nothing works. I'm stiff as a board. All except Dick Johnson there." He sat on a bench and tried to cry but that didn't even work properly, a few tears dripping from his left ear. "And who'd want to be with me anyway? Nobody I'd want to be with. Look at this!"

Margaret Truman came careening around a corner, arms working furiously, battling decay. She looked at Beasley briefly, five seconds passed and then she screamed and crashed into a light pole, breaking her nose but not her dentures.

Joe Beasley's situation, as it happened, was the last straw for Jesus Christ, who had been planning a big return to coincide with the hundredth anniversary of Woodstock.

"Here I am hanging around in the Kingdom Come of Monotony the last couple millennia. I was supposed to get cosmic understanding but that didn't happen and actually, I don't think You know much more than I do. At this point I'd probably rather not know anyway. Here I thought at least I was something special because I got resurrected and now look at this! Joe Beasley, fifty something walking penis not a genius comes back and not only that, he gets to stay on Earth! I tell you it's demoralizing. What was all that about??? I'd rather have just waited for the musical."

"They wouldn't have cast you in the lead anyway. You don't look the part."

"What do You mean I don't look the part. I am the part."

"Sure, My son, but they think you were white, like Me. You might have made it as Judas."

Tiring of Jesus' whining, God said, "Look. You were the big cheese for quite a while. Technology was bound to catch up with us. Anyway look at him. Nobody's going to build a religion around that. Hell. Nobody would even try to seduce that. People want a savior that looks like he at least has connections. The name alone will stop him. How far do you think you'd have gotten as Joe Beasley? Beasleyanity? They wouldn't even have gotten the Inquisition off the ground."

"I still don't see why You couldn't leave me alone over there. I was doing alright. The world was ripe for me. Did You ever think I might want to stay around and enjoy the fruit of my... our labor? Like a farmer tending his corn? Maybe I could have had a wife and kids. But no, You had to have Your big scene. Had to meddle.

"Alright, that's it. When are you going to get it through your thick skull that I had nothing to do with that? Things just turned out that way. You ought to be grateful I at least brought you back. If there's anybody predestining things, it sure isn't Me. I had actually forgotten all about you by then, you know. You could have stayed forever but you screwed up. Seemed like a good ending though.

Looking back with the long view, doesn't seem so important anymore."

"Well that's good to know. I'll tell You this – I didn't like it very much. You're always going back to Earth. Why can't I? I would like to taste Earth again."

"Where would you want to go?"

"Oh, I don't know. Maybe Florida. And another thing I'd like to know – why do I have a last name and You don't? Doesn't a boy usually get his father's last name? Where'd You come up with "Christ?"

"It went good with Christianity." God was silent for an indeterminate period. Then He said, "I too have a last name. I didn't think you'd want it. You'll have to be satisfied with that."

God sighed (and blew out five suns, in one breath wiping out the beginnings of life on one planet and an ancient civilization on another). "I hope you're not starting to believe that stuff about how you're God because I resurrected you. I was surprised even the Americans were gullible enough to buy that marketing stunt, the old switcheroo. Of course they learned that trick and did it themselves with those Muslim guys. But that was pretty simple. You've seen one Muslim..... But for you it's not logical. You simply can't be the thing that made you. You're just My halfbreed son who's a lot more popular than I am now because of that stupid Old Testament. If I ever get my hands on the s.o.b. that wrote that libelous depiction of Me as a jealous, vengeful god ...scared a lot of people off. It was distasteful but to tone down My image and sometimes, as we all know, image is everything, I copulated with a woman human. I was in the Dark Continent at the time and, well, there you are. That's it. If you liked being human so much, you're lucky she was the one to get pregnant and not the gorilla. Although... it would have to be a really slow day for them to crucify a gorilla. I actually can't see them doing it. I don't know why, don't know exactly why."

"Too strong," Jesus said curtly. "It's because gorillas are too strong."

"Yes. Yes, that must be it. Too strong to crucify.

"Like Superman."

"You know that's not a bad slogan if you had something to sell with it. "Oh yeah, and there was the elephant. Anyway the genesis of your existence was a public relations move and all these options you go on about aren't included with that. I could ask 'What have you done for me lately?' and your answer is going to be a resounding 'Not much.' So I wouldn't push it if I were you."

Jimmy Buffett, the only human ever allowed to be on Earth and in Heaven, floated up, nodded at Jesus, yelled "Good God Almighty!" and started performing God's favorite song, "Volcano."

God brightened. "I love that song," he said to Jesus. "It's so stupid. Just doesn't make any sense."

Jesus went off and sulked. What if everyone thinks Joe Beasley is my second coming? That would be pretty much it for Christianity. All that torture for nothing because of some high-tech heathens living in the dirt that I didn't even know about. And Dear Old Good God Almighty couldn't care less about what happens to my religion. I can just hear the Jews. "Mosul tov. This is it? What we've been waiting for? This is what's going to make the Germans worth it? I want a refund."

In defiance of his Father, Jesus beamed Superman flying style to Earth, The Villages in particular to deal with The Beasley Factor.

This is what I get for taking so long to come back, he thought, zooming covertly to his destination. Not very good at steering and unable to get lessons from his Father, he hoped he could land without being noticed.

Jimmy Oldson had just returned from a hard day unearthing the proclivities of The Villages and no closer to breaking the Beasley case wide open. As he showered off the day with Irish Spring, Maxine had removed all her clothes and supinely waited to surprise him when he entered the bedroom. Expecting his lover to be up to something naughty, Oldson teased her by prolonging his shower. Maxine fell asleep. She awoke to the sensation of someone descending upon her. Jimmy walked in the room very disappointed to notice she was under a naked black man.

The reporter felt horror such as he never could imagine. "Maxine!" he yelled and staggered backwards.

She threw Jesus off her and cried, "Oh Jimmy. I don't know where he came from."

"Oh, that's a good one," Oldson retorted.

Jesus sprang up to explain it was just a bad landing but Jimmy Oldson, though a reporter for a great metropolitan newspaper, was not listening. Experiencing rage for the first time, he closed inspired hands around Jesus' throat. Meanwhile Maxine dialed 911. Jesus managed to squeak out, "Okay, I surrender."

When Jimmy eased his grip, the holy man sped out the room and out the door. Two neighbors and a Croation poodle saw a black man wearing a loin cloth streak from the Oldson apartment and down the stairs. All except the pooch punched in 911. Fast becoming the only reporter that Verry White needed, Oldson had his headline for the next issue.

19

L ittle would Joe Beasley imagine he had become the envy of Jesus, not at all considering himself resurrected. He hadn't even much of a chance to consider himself dead. Joe didn't know what to think except that maybe he needed to talk to someone. A scientist? A priest? A talk Show host? The President? Actually his mom. That is who he really wanted to talk to but she already had departed the mortal coil in the widely accepted manner and was inaccessible to him in his present state. Then he remembered he had a house. Since all his appetites had been removed by the embalmer, everything was in the house that he needed. He thought he might go home and lie down on the bed, maybe fall asleep and wake up to learn this had been only a really stupid dream. Through the night he walked zombie speed only to find a realtor lock on the front door. Goddammit having become his go-to response to everything lately, he uttered it once more and he was surprised to hear a sublimely gentle reply.

"Why do you always state this command? You only encourage Him, you know."

The lock fell off and the door opened. "Come in," soothed the voice.

"Did you know," it continued, "there never is a moment when someone isn't praying that on your planet? In fact there is a lot of overlap. It is the only constant message God receives from His flock. And then you wonder why things go as they do."

"Who the Hell are you and what are you doing in my house?"

"Being a unified prayer 'God dammit' drowns out the other ones, making a virtual force field that blocks them out.. God knows people are praying for cars and wealth and healing, He just can't hear it most of the time and He certainly can't tell who is axing for what. So God dammit takes over."

"I don't give a shit about God Dammit or Mary Poppins or anybody else right now. I just want you the Hell out of my house or I'm calling the cops."

Joe tries to collapse onto the couch but it's not there anymore and he crumples to the terrazzo floor.

"Oops. Sorry. I should have foreseen that and returned your couch in time." By raising a hand the visitor stands Joe up and them deposits him on his old couch.

"Alright. That was weird. How did that happen?"

"All in good time."

"Are you another one of these underground assholes?"

"Underground is not my realm, nor, I hope, is asshole. But then again, I might think about annexing the Underworld. That would show the Heavenly Father a thing or two."

"Alright. I'm gonna assume you're a colored guy who thinks he might be Jesus. And after that snappy little thing you just did, I wouldn't rule it out. I'm only willing to think that because I just recently turned into a zombie, so at this point anything goes. Are you Jesus? Because I really hope you are. I could use a friend."

"Well, they call me Jesus of Nazareth, pilgrim."

"That narrows you down to either Jesus or John Wayne."

"I'm certainly not John Wayne."

"Tell me this. How come nobody knew you were colored? All the pictures you're in, you're white."

Jesus sighed, musing "and these are my flock.

"They didn't have cameras back then and if they did, the whole thing probably would have become just another documentary, if that. With luck I'd have been right there with Haile Sellasee. You can't start up a religion when the watchword is 'Seeing is believing.' But let me get to the point of my visit. I came back, prematurely I might add, because of you and your half-assed return from being dead. Simon and Garfunkel was close enough and now this."

"If you're Jesus, how come you said 'half- assed?'

"I lived here for several years, you know. Just listen to me. Word of this gets out, I might as well fold my tent and go to Mars. You, such as you are, will be the new Messiah. And honestly, far more appropriate than me."

"You're telling me there's gonna be a whole new wave of merchandising? With me on the cross?"

"The crosses won't even have to be entirely retooled. I'm not wearing much anyway and the face is arbitrary as long as it's white, which you are."

Joe nodded and a few eyelashes fluttered to the floor. "As long as they're changing it, I'll bet I could sell customized crucifixes, make a mint. People could order their own face on there."

"You sure don't make it easy, Joe. But yeah. Go for it. One thing for sure, you're not going to enjoy it as you are, going around like a living crucifixion. So I have a deal for you. You let me stuff your soul and general being into my body. Just think of it. You'll be the only negro living in this community of fifty-year old nymphomaniacs."

"That's just it. I'd be black. That's probably worse than a white zombie."

"I think you will find otherwise to be the case. You're not getting Louis Armstrong or Bill Cosby here. Look at me! I certainly did alright a couple thousand years ago. Little piece of midnight broke off in their lives, I got tired beating them off. That's probably why I seemed so peaceful all the time. Just keep thinking white, behaving as if you're white and the rest will follow. There is nothing more alluring to a white woman than an oreo. In return for all this, I take your ridiculous casing back to Heaven where it won't matter anyway and cool my heels until the 100th anniversary of Woodstock when I'll return and reverse the process. Then you can just go ahead and die like you're supposed to. See you in Heaven. If you're a good boy. Waddaya say??"

"I dunno. You put a lot of miles on that chassis. Sure

it looks good but that's how they fool ya. Great body, why's it so cheap? You have to wonder what's going on under the hood."

Jesus was trying to stay calm, like Jesus, hold down the pressure building within. Slowly, deliberately he said, "You're not buying a car. And look at yourself, what I'm swapping you even for. How can this not be a great deal for you?"

Beasley looked him up and down, walked around behind him, did everything but kick the tires. "Wow. I'm used to, like, the devil coming around and making deals, not Jesus. You hold all the cards. You don't have to make deals."

"No, you're making that common mistake of confusing me with my Father. You know what happened. Do you think I would have chosen that? Would you?"

"I gotta think about this. You could be the devil, I sign on the dotted line and then my goose is really cooked. I play it safe, face the music and stay like this, the way God for some perfectly good reason meant me to be, at least when I do die, I'll go to heaven."

Oh Wooweee, Jesus thought, you should be careful etc. "Okay, what do I have to do to prove I'm the son of God?"

"How about healing me?"

"Nice try. I want something out of this too."

"Alright. Burn down a synagogue."

"This is a test, isn't it? I agree, I am the devil, I refuse I must be Jesus, right?"

"I don't know. Walk on the swimming pool."

"How pedestrian. You think the devil can't do that? He could just make you think he did that. For that matter he could make you do it. Let me axe you this. How about just believing. That can go a long way. Probably grease your way into Heaven."

"Guess I got nothing to lose. I sure don't want to stay like this."

So there it was, the next day, transformation wrought, embalmed zombie Jesus soon to be on his way back to Heaven, hoping maybe the omnipotent one hadn't noticed he'd gone.

"Say Jesus," Joe Beasley said, "Long as I've got you here, can I ask you a question?"

"Shoot."

"I suppose people are always asking you this but what's the meaning of life?"

"Oh Joe, you know very well the answer to that. You just don't realize you do. Like many people, you think there is more."

"Okay, yeah, I see." Joe nodded sadly.

"Jesus Christ!" God boomed on the return of His son. "What happened to you!?! You looked better the other time."

"Oh, nothing. As usual. This is a costume."

"A costume eh? Take it off."

"Well, I..."

"You know I sent Lucifer to Hell for disobeying Me. Is that what you want Me to do with you? Send you to

Hell?"

"You've been threatening me with that since I was five. You got me on the cross with it. But you know what? I don't believe in Hell anymore. So go ahead, do Your worst. Send me to Hell. Go on."

Looks like Jesus might need some almighty lessons in diplomacy. Meantime Joe (Shaft) Beasley was feeling a whole lot better. In fact he was leaping around like a Mexican jumping bean in a hot skillet.

Beasley was starting to appreciate his new position. "Now this is more like it. So what if I'm black. I wonder how fast I can run; and he shot off down the road, just in time for a Sumter County Sheriff's Deputy to spot him. "Looks like we got our rapist, 10-4."

20

Some American Africans from Leesburg were corralled for the line-up and Maxine Falderall and Jimmy Oldson had no trouble identifying the one that had been on top of her.

Beasley of course had no recollection of being atop Ms. Falderall. Nor could he adequately explain who he was or where he'd come from, or most of all, why he was a Chicago White Sox fan; partly because he barely believed it himself. His true account of recent events was of use to him only to back up an insanity plea. Certainly nobody believed he was Joe Beasley. "That damn, er... darn Jesus," he fumed. "He didn't mention anything about this happening, did he?"

Then he recognized the upside to this. He was relieved of all concerns besides his situation – elections, code enforcement, old friends who never again would acknowledge him, the American League all meant nothing to him now. He was along just for the ride.

Percival Mason got a call from Joe Beasley. Mason

insisted Beasley tell him the whole truth so, with some reluctance Beasley did.

When Beasley was finished, the celebrated lawyer said, "You're sure that's it. There's nothing else."

Beasley nodded over the phone.

"No demon from the fifth dimension turning you into a flying hippopotamus and then throwing you into the Pentagon for example."

"No," Beasley deadpanned, "nothing like that. Although I am halfway expecting it."

"You're not claiming to have seen Bigfoot teaching children the guitar, a talking Cuban sandwich riding a dead horse or a Fox News host with a shred of dignity."

"Absolutely not."

"I don't suppose you have any witnesses or photographic or video confirmation of this outlandish story."

"Nope."

"Alright, I'll take the case. I've had worse. But keep me informed of any new developments."

"You do believe me, don't you, Mr Mason?"

"Yes I do but then I'm used to longshots. It's not going to be easy to get a jury to swallow it. In fact I'm probably the only lawyer that could. Is there any chance you can get Jesus to testify? I don't have to tell you what a credibility boost that would be."

"Jesus. No, I don't think so. It's not like I have his phone number."

"He's not on Instantgram or anything like that?"

142

"Not that I know of."

"Then I suggest you start praying."

"I really don't think he would be much help anyway. He looks really bad. People wouldn't even believe who he is."

"Do you believe he is who he claims to be?"

"It's all I've got," Mr. Mason.

"Still, try praying. You never know what that might yield. After all, he got you in this fix in the first place."

"Actually it all started with those assholes in the ground."

Mason looked thoughtful. "Tell you what. I'll put Paul Drake on it, see what he can come up with. If this guy really is the Christ, and he really did try to rape Ms. Falderall while he was still black, I don't think he'd let you take the fall. That wouldn't be the Christian thing to do... and I'll have Paul see if he can flush out one of these mole-people."

"I don't know how to thank you."

Mason clapped him on the back. "Don't even try yet."

Paul Drake got himself a golf cart size extra large and putted into the east side of The Villages just to nose around, see what the word is on the street. The word turned out to be "Ex-Lax." Besides that he found the citizenry mostly comparing their histories of disease and operations, each hoping to top the other. Then he noticed a man fishing alone from the boardwalk at Lake Humpter Landing.

Drake leaned on the rail a few feet away looking at the water. "Catching any?"

Barney Jenkins removed hydrilla from his artificial worm. "Another one, eh?"

"Another what?"

"Reporter. What else? Doing a piece on fishing in The Villages? 'Cause I can save you some time. It sucks."

"My name's Pete Ducker. I'm thinking about moving here. There's been some strange stuff reported and I'm just trying to get some info on it. "

"Here's some info for you. You should buzz off."

"You wouldn't happen to know anything about people getting sucked into the ground around here would you?"

"You want to know if we have quicksand in The Villages?"

"Not exactly. Apparently it can happen anywhere, maybe even out of your house."

"Matter of fact, this other reporter was blabbering at me and he suddenly disappeared. Then he reappeared. I don't know where the Hell he went but maybe he wouldn't shut up so they sent him back. You oughta try the same thing. Without the reappear part."

"Whatsa matter? Didn't get your Ex-Lax fix?"

"No but you ever see a guy change his colostomy bag?"

"I haven't but I've probably seen worse. Let's go."

"Ah, forget it. I don't even have one."

"Maybe someday." Drake pointed. "Check out that guy's great dane over there taking a dump. Maybe that'll prime your pump."

"Don't worry. My pump is plenty primed."

The P.I. kicked his feet back and leaned his considerable bulk a little harder on the rail and became philosophical. "I wonder why people don't give dogs colostomy bags. That way they wouldn't have to take them on walks and humiliate themselves scooping up piles in front of everybody. They could just monitor the bag and when it's full, change it out in the privacy of their home."

"You know, Pucker, I think you're onto something. Why don't you go somewhere and invent it?"

"Mind if I make a cast?"

"Not a good idea. If you caught something I'd have to kill you."

Perry Mason and his secretary were sitting around imagining each other naked when Paul Drake entered.

"Alright Paul, what have you learned?"

"For a start, most of the people living there have had cancer or are hoping to get it soon. Also there is a shortage of laxatives since Covid, with a flourishing black market for Ex-Lax, and gold shoes means the wearer is available."

"Available for what, Paul?" Della Street asked.

"Hijinks."

"Oh."

"Anybody connecting Beasley with the black market?"

"No, but half a dozen locals hit me up for some."

"You must look the part," Della Street said.

"I'll ignore that. And as it happens, the black market and your client are the only black things there."

"An entirely white population?"

"Entirely."

"Well, none of that will help Mr. Beasley, I'm afraid."

"Oh, one other thing, it's probably nothing but this crusty old coot said something about a reporter disappearing and then reappearing."

"That could be the break we're looking for, Paul. Did you get this crispy codger's name?"

"Well, no, but I think I can find him. He's the Don Rickles of The Villages."

"I've just had an idea. Della, put out a call for anybody who knew Mr. Beasley. Someone might know something that only Beasley would know."

"You know, you're right."

"So that's it, Maxine. This black guy claims to be Joe Beasley, says he got sucked into the ground, then got spat back out embalmed as a zombie and Jesus got jealous and came down to swap bodies with him. But for some reason Jesus landed on you when he got here."

"That's the craziest thing I ever heard," Maxine said.

"Yeah it is pretty crazy. Are you sure you never saw him before?"

"Jimmy!#!"

"Okay, okay. Is it crazier than everybody getting pregnant with Donald Trump?"

"Yes, I think so. But what if it's true? It seems like anything can happen these days, in The Villages."

146

"I sure got transported somewhere. They said I was under The Villages."

"Maybe you should tell the judge about it."

"I'd rather see how the trial goes. I get labeled as a nut, there goes my job. I'm a family man now, got to think about you and your nameless offspring."

"Jimmy! You keep saying things like that and we may have to break up."

"Aw, don't sweat it Maxine. You know I just like to get you riled."

"Maybe we shouldn't name it. It might be very liberating not to have a name. Just free, nothing to answer to, not another Tom, Dick or Falarianjavospin. It might be very grateful to us someday."

"Hey – maybe Donald Trump got how he is because he got named after a bad-tempered duck."

"With no pants."

"What if we get rid of our names? Then we could be the nameless family. Just kind of float around." Oldson unwrapped a Tootsie Pop. "You want one?"

"No thank you." Maxine smiled sweetly. "I must watch my girlish figure. So you'll watch it."

"True or not the only chance Black Beasley has is an insanity plea."

"Perry Mason would never allow that. He always goes for the win."

"That's on tv where there's a script. He may find it's not so easy in the Sumter County Courthouse."

"Maybe I should go talk to him, find out if it really is

my Joe. I could ask about things only Joe could know."

"What do you mean 'my Joe?'"

"Well Jimmy, I knew him long before I knew you."

"Yeah, Maxine, but it just makes me, I don't know..."

"Jealous?"

"Yeah I guess that's it."

"Well there's nothing wrong with that."

21

An emergency meeting has called together the Central Florida KKK. "Alright, Wayne, they's sayin' a nigger did a old white lady right here in Lady Lake."

"That makes me sick of my stummick."

"Now we done seed the only nigger fer a hunnerd miles drivin that mail truck."

Wayne Clueless started jumping up and down. "He gots to be the one, Curtis. He gots to be."

"Dang, Wayne, why you allus missin the point?"

Pouting, Clueless whined, "Wha'd I do wrong this time, Curtis?"

"Well Wayne, try and think about it. It's niggers in general done it. So what's it matter who done the deed, slong as we lynch a nigger fer it? Shoot. They already done arrested some jigaboo tourist. Don't you see? It's open season again."

Wayne blurted, "I get it, Curtis. It's like scoochin a roach in the kitchen. You don't think about is this the one

149

got in the jam jar. It's jes one less roach. Yeeha. We got us a lynchin."

"It's agonna be easy, Wayne. We don't got to worry about no feds now. We get a few more of the boys up here and next time that coon mailqueer comes in our office with the mail, we hit it over the head. We keeps it on ice til 'bout two o'clock in the mornin', then we goes out and strings it up.

"Uh, Wayne, you didn't jest pee your pants did you?"

"Kind of."

"Don't fret none about it. I think I jest shat mine."

"Curtis, ain't they sposed to be awake when you lynches 'em?"

"Thet was the good old days, Wayne. We ain't quite back there yet."

"But that's half the fun in it – thinkin bout them knowin what's about to happen to 'em."

"Don't worry, Wayne. This works out there'll be more a-comin and mebbe we kin do 'er right."

Wayne Wagner said,"Curtis, what ifn we git caught? They's probly laws agin it."

"They won't be nothin' to git caught fer. Gonna be a free and clear sewerside. Gonna pin a note on it."

Four days later residents of The Villages and tourists received the sight of a new body, already black, as if by magic hanging beside the original miracle effigy. Most observers really didn't know much what to make of the pairing. After a few hours the organic nature of the newcomer became apparent and the sheriff was called.

150

"Lookit here – a note!" Deputy Fife yelled. "Listen to this: 'Goodby Crool Werld.'"

"Looks like he killed himself alright," said the sheriff.

The county coroner agreed.

Americans for a Better Trump quietly closed up shop and slithered back down to Taft covered in glory.

As the victim was not a Villageer, and a suicide to boot, the story was off the intrepid Oldson's beat. There was some immediate public outcry against an outlyer having the gall to dispatch himself in The Villages and the bad taste to do it adjacent the miracle effigy; but that quickly simmered down.

God had confined Jesus to his bedroom, but couldn't resist letting him out for a look. "Look at this," He said, pointing at The Villages, "They did it again. This time they hung you and I didn't even know about it, much less arrange it."

Jesus looked in dismay. "That's not me, you know, it's a metaphor - some other poor schmuck in the wrong place at the wrong time."

"Well, they probably thought it was you. Why does this keep happening?"

"I don't know Man. How should I know? I'm just King of the Jews. Why don't You know? You're the One Who's supposed to know everything."

"Look son, all kids think their father can do anything. I keep trying to tell you, I'm not omniscient. My strong suit is what I don't know, not what I know. I don't know way more than anyone else doesn't know. 'I think therefore I am.' What moron said that? 'I think that's all there is' is a lot closer to the mark. We'll never know anything because there is nothing to know; only things not to know. Expanded awareness just reveals more of those. Do you understand? I'm only godlike compared to something as pitiful as life."

"I guess I'm stuck with this body, huh?"

God surveyed his progeny and couldn't help laughing. "At least you look white now. If you go back maybe they won't kill you."

"Let me axe You this. Why did Superman get to be white, got super powers, no crucifixion, just has fun on Earth, actually got his own tv show?"

"Alright, you want the truth, you're going to get it. As for this demise of yours you're always whining about – that never happened. There's a reason they call it cruci-fiction. I just put out lots of propaganda with your people taking the rap, of course. You eventually bought into it like everybody else. I'm not Mr. Nice God but I wouldn't crucify My own boy. Humans aren't that important."

"What?!?*!? Why do people get stigmata if I never got crucified?"

"I wonder about that myself. Maybe it's a miracle. Anyway it plays well with the faithful. You never minded it, right?"

"So me walking around after I got buried, what was that, holograms?"

"Holograms?? We didn't have that kind of technology.

It just really didn't happen. Any of it."

Jesus collapsed into stunned silence. It's all a lie, he thought. All of it. Everything I've thought for thousands of years. I'm nothing special, just the same thing I always was, never came back from the dead, never even been dead. Joe Beasley does have me beat. I must get back there, must stop him, must save good old time religion because it is a good thing, good for my flock, whether I'm a phony or not.

"And while I'm at it, let me tell you about that tv show," God carried on to Jesus who was no longer listening. "It was a huge embarrassment and I was glad everybody thought I had nothing to do with it. As for Superman being white, it had something to do with me and Wonder Woman being white. I couldn't resist. There she was lying naked out in a field. I got her right through the invisible man, which is why he hasn't been heard from since, although only blind people really miss him. And that doesn't make me homosexual. You can go through a guy as long as you end up in a woman. And as human women go, Va va Voom!"

God noticed an albino man step from the shadows and gaze up at the remaining effigy of Whitey, still black. "Hey look. It's My old sidekick Mike. I forgot all about him." Pence backed away and started running. God threw a banana peel in front of him but Pence missed it and kept going until he got to Johnny Rocket's.

22

The jury consisted of three Mike Pence look-alikes and eight white women chosen basically for being the most wide awake during the selection process. The first female judge in Sumter County history, recently arrived from Ohio, Pontius Violet presided over the rape trial. She said, "Order is in the court."

Prosecutor Cheeselton Burger presented his simple, damning case against the black man claiming to be the dead white man Joe Beasley: Maxine Falderall testified to awakening nude with the naked defendant atop her. Jimmy Oldson testified to seeing Miss Falderall throw him off her, and two neighbors said they saw the man in question streaking from the Oldson apartment. To top it off, the accused, though pleading not guilty, admitted all this was probably true because Jesus admitted it, actually thought it was kind of funny. Even Perry Mason, the pundits were saying, wasn't going to overcome that, and his perfect record finally was doomed.

Come time for the defense to present its case, which

was to explain that the defendant's current body had been flown naked by Jesus Christ to The Villages from Heaven and accidentally landed in Lady Lake on Ms. Falderall and the Christ swapped bodies with the zombified Joe Beasley, innocent though now appearing in the guilty body. Perry Mason leaned toward the defendant. "I don't think they bought it, Joe. They think they've heard it all before. "It's up to you now. I'm going to bring a parade of women through here who claim to have known you. They've all attested to some unique feature on their bodies that no black man has seen but Joe Beasley has. If you can corroborate this, it will at least prove you used to be white."

"But Mr. Mason, I don't know what woman goes with what feature. There were too many. Just too many faces. Hell. One of them had an extra teat. I remember that but I couldn't give you a face to go with it."

"If you don't mind my asking, where was the third one?"

"Not where you'd expect it to be."

"Alright." Mason stared at his client. "If you can nail just that one, I think we're home free."

Emily Barnhorst had a litany of unique features mostly due to her uncommon age. Beasley was horrified when she took the stand, vehemently denying to his lawyer that there was any way he would have seen any of her anomalies unless she just walked around town naked. And even then, he wouldn't have looked.

Perry Mason addressed Pontius Violet. "Your honor it is clear this is a hostile witness and I wish to treat her as such."

"Your wish is granted."

"Ms. Barnhorst, have you ever walked around town naked?"

"What??"

"Mr. Mason," Violet cautioned, "I hope you know where you're going with this."

"I hope I do too," the famed lawyer responded.

"The witness will answer the question."

"Well ...not in the daytime."

A rumble ran through the spectators. "I knew it," Jim Baxter whispered to Bud Tinsley, "That was her."

Mason pressed Ms. Barnhorst. "Are you certain it was Joe Beasley you were with? Isn't it possible you just wished it was the highly acclaimed Mr. Beasley?"

"Of course I'm certain. What kind of a girl do you think I am?"

"How did this tryst come about?"

Emily squirmed a little in the witness stand. "I think I was feeding some ducks at Lake Humpter. Joe came over and asked if he could have some bread too, so he could feed them. He said he wanted to get on the good side of ducks in case God turns out to be one. He said, "I like to cover all my bases, if you know what I mean and then he winked."

"He winked? Lake Humpter is known for volatile weather. Are you sure a breeze didn't spring up, lodging a dust particle in his eye?"

"Oh no, once you've seen the Beasley wink, there's no forgetting it. And it's no dust particle."

156

A murmur of affirmation rippled through the crowd. Pontius Violet struck with her gavel. "If there are any more such demonstrations, I'll instruct the bailiff to clear the courtroom."

"What happened then?"

"Like I said, once you've been winked at..."

The defendant grabbed his lawyer by the coat sleeve. "I'm telling you I never winked at that woman. Never!"

"Ms. Barnhorst, even assuming all this is accurate, how could you be sure this man was Joe Beasley?"

"If I wasn't sure before, I was darn sure after."

The courtroom burst into laughter. Said Sally Struthers, "This is the Joe Beasley Appreciation Day we never had."

Pontius Violet slammed down her gavel. "This is your last warning!"

"Your Honor, I'd like to declare this an unreliable witness."

"Mr. Mason, I see no justification for that. You are the one who chose this unorthodox method of finding the truth. You'll have to stick with it."

"I OBJECT!"

"Mr. Mason, you can't object at me. Please proceed."

Mason looked at his client. "Just remember one thing, Joe. I've never lost. There's more here at stake than your Beasley life. There's my perfect record."

Beasley looked with irony upon his lawyer and said. "I'll try my hardest for you. Then he stood and ventured, "Well, there's a real cute wrinkle across her belly."

Barnhorst tipped her noggin coquettishly, then she slowly looked up and nodded. "That's Joe Beasely alright. Ain't no colored ever saw that."

Prosecutor Cheeselton Burger stood. "I move that conclusion be stricken from the record.

"Strike it." Pontius Violet blew on her hand.

"I also move that ..."

"Yes, Mr. Burger?"

"Oh, never mind."

Mason stood. "Your honor we can save the court time if we allow Ms. Barnhorst's testimony to stand for all the women of the Villages."

"Saving time would be good. But we should hear from one more to corroborate this witness."

"A moment to confer with my client please."

"Don't take forever. Remember the point of this is to save time."

"Joe, do any of those women look familiar?"

"They all do, Mr. Mason. Vaguely. You know, I've been through a lot lately."

"Well, stick with generalities."

"Maxine Falderall to the stand." The crowd drew in a collective breath.

"I have a question for the defendant," Ms. Falderall stated forthrightly.

Perry Mason whispered to his client, "Do you recognize this one?"

Beasley shook his head. "Never saw her before in my

life."

"Here is my question," said the determined Falderall, "If that was you, Joe, why did you have to wait so long?"

"Don't you see?" he sputtered, "that wasn't me. That was Jesus, before we switched bodies."

"Alright," Maxine said, "If that's Joe Beasley sitting there, he alone can answer this question:" She took a moment to compose herself, then inhaled deeply. "How many times did we have sex?"

"I don't keep score like that," Joe said, futilely trying to command the high ground.

"Answer the witness," the judge instructed.

The defendant looked helplessly at his lawyer. "Go ahead, Joe. Roll the dice on my career. I'd say stick with a low number."

Joe Beasley inhaled deeply, perhaps some of the last free air he would breathe. "Somebody pretty as you, I hope at least three times."

Had it been a white man answering, the spectators would have tittered. Instead it was received with stony silence. Maxine shook her head. "The answer is zero. You're not Joe Beasley. You're not my Joe."

The courtroom exhaled as one.

Pontius Violet gaveled again. "It seems we're at an impasse and it's about lunchtime. We will take one more witness for the tiebreaker."

Mason leaned in again on his client. "I never should have taken your stupid rape case. I should have stuck with murder cases. There should be a limit to what I'll believe.

Now my perfect record is in the hands of some hormonal woman."

The judge said, "To serve both time and fairness, the next witness is me. Tell me Mr. Beasley, if you're really him. What do I have that distinguishes me?"

Both lawyers started to object but just looked at each other and sat down. "Jesus," Joe said, having lost all hope. He racked his brain, trying to make a connection, straining to remember even doing Pontius Violet. Seems like I'd remember a judge. Maybe I didn't know she was. Too bad, he thinks, I would have liked knowing that.

The courtroom was silent as the defendant rose. "I don't know," he said in despair. "Three tits?"

The general hilarity in the room could not be contained. When the judge finally managed to gavel it away she said, "I don't know that he's Joe Beasley but at one point in his life, this man was white. That much is certain." Half the people in the courtroom vomited when Pontius Violet stood and lifted her robe. She gaveled. "We'll adjourn for lunch. Be back here by one."

Back in court Perry Mason addressed Pontius Violet: "Having established that the defendant, the spirit, the soul of the man inside the skin we have put on trial, is an identity separate from the black body manifested here, we must decide which one we are trying. Are we trying the body, as so often happens, or the soul? This is a rare case where they cannot be caught in the same net. It is our contention that physical recognition of the body in no way impugns the soul occupying it now. We plan to show that it was not Joe Beasley but Jesus Christ attempting the rape of

Maxine Falderall; and at the time this crime was being perpetrated, Joe Beasley was a very white zombie.

"I call Joe Beasley to the stand."

Prosecutor Cheeselton Burger rocketed from his seat. With strained voice he cried, "You honor, Joe Beasley is dead. He was found dead, identified as dead and declared dead and he's had a very popular funeral. Joe Beasley is deader than disco and everyone knows it. Of all the goofy stunts Perry Mason has pulled over the years, this is the worst. Dead people may vote but they cannot be called as witnesses. And while the defendant was alive, he looked nothing like this man now claiming to be him."

Perry Mason stood. "The defendant believes himself to be Joe Beasley and in fact the entire efficacy of the defense rests upon this. To disallow it now would be to declare him guilty before the trial is finished. Let me further cite Miracle on 29th St. in which the existence and location of Santa Claus was recognized by the court based on the delivery by no less an entity than the United States Postal Service of letters so addressed."

"Does the defendant have in his possession any mail addressed to Joe Beasley?"

Mason looked at Beasley shaking his head. "No, Your Honor, he has not. Joe Beasley stopped getting mail before he occupied Jesus' body - except for mail labeled 'Occupant', sent to 114 Yabadabadoo Dr., the address of Joe Beasley, mail picked up while briefly occupying that house where he met Jesus Christ, which I now present to the court."

The judge examined the envelope. "It's good for him

that it was generically addressed," Judge Violet stated, "or we would be adding the charge of mail theft. I'm going to allow it."

"What?!? Has the world gone mad?" Burger blurted, blasting up and throwing his pencil into the air before slumping back into his seat.

Jesus' body stood and Joe Beasley strode to the witness stand where he was sworn in. Perry Mason said, "Joe, where did you grow up? "

"Why, Bettendorf, Iowa."

"Please tell the court what it was like growing up black in the almost completely white Iowa."

"Mr. Mason, I couldn't tell you. You see, I was as white as Paul Drake then."

Cheeselton Burger pulled the trigger on his finger, blowing his brains out.

"What color were you on the day Maxine Falderall was accosted by a black man in her bed?"

"Still white."

"So you had no involvement whatsoever in this situation until Jesus, having escaped the scene of the crime, sought you out to trade bodies, thereby ensuring his exoneration. And then and only then did you take on the appearance of the real perpetrator of the crime, Jesus Christ."

"Absolutely right."

"Mr. Beasley, you are a mid-westerner, is that not true?"

"That's right."

"And were you taught mid-western values by your parents?"

"To the tune of a hickory stick." The spectators, mid-westerners all, chuckled appreciatively.

"And one of these values was always to tell the truth?"

"Yes, sir."

"So in spite of the unusual nature of your story, truth is what you are compelled by your upbringing to tell now, isn't it?"

"Yes, sir," Beasley stated solidly. "I could make something up that would sound a lot more likely, although darned if I know what it would be, given my circumstances, but it wouldn't be the truth."

"Sometimes the truth isn't the easiest path to take, is it?"

"You can say that again."

"Sometimes truth isn't the easiest path to take, is it?"

"Mr. Mason," Judge Violet scolded, "this is a courtroom, not a comedy club."

"I'm sorry, your Honor, I just couldn't help it.

"Joe," Mason continued, "Tell exactly what happened."

And that's what he did. Even this select audience had a hard time swallowing the subterranean part but they were willing to try; black Jesus was a bridge too far. It could be seen on their faces. The judge said, "Mr. Mason, are you sure you aren't doing your client a disservice by not pleading guilty by reason of insanity?"

Just then Paul Drake burst into the courtroom and

163

rushed down the aisle with the bailiff grabbing at him.

Perry Mason asked the judge for a minute. "Sure but don't keep me hanging."

Drake was about to burst. "Perry I just came from Seismology R Us. Look at these readings."

Mason perused the pictures. "I'm not really seeing anything, Paul."

"It's not a snapshot of some bikini at the beach. You have to know what to look for."

"And what we're looking for is here?"

"Yep."

Mason approached the bench. "I'd like to submit these images into evidence, pictures that prove my client's story: radar readings showing people living beneath the surface of The Villages."

His finger wasn't loaded so Burger was still alive and on his feet again. "Your Honor, that's hearsay and as such inadmissible as evidence."

Drake said, "Ed Asner, owner of the company, will be here in fifteen minutes."

The judge gaveled. "We'll break for a half hour."

"Paul," Perry Mason said behind the courthouse, sucking large on a doobie before handing it to the ace p.i, "they're sure these images actually represent underground people?"

"Absolutely. You should have seen how excited they were."

"You realize that if this part of my client's story is true, it leaves the door wide open for the rest of it to be true."

164

"I've already thought about that."

"The ramifications would have worldwide impact," Mason stated gravely.

"You know it. God's real and Jesus is black. That'd be enough to resurrect the newspaper industry." Mason started giggling and Paul caught it and soon they were sitting on the ground laughing off their butts.

"Not quite," Mason said, recovering himself. "According to my client, Jesus is now a white zombie. I'm wondering if we ought to just let it go, plead Beasley nuts. If we don't we could throw the civilized world into chaos."

"I wouldn't worry about that Perry. People can get used to anything. A month from now this'll all be back page and Jesus'll be doing Shroud of Turin infomercials. Besides, we have your record to consider. Perry Mason losing a case – now that would unglue the fabric of society."

"Well, Paul, then maybe I should lose one."

"Yeah, there is that."

With no cell phone reception in The Villages, Jimmy Oldson sped out the courtroom to the nearest pay phone. He got stuck on whom to call first, his love, his mother or his editor. "Hey buddy. Use it or lose it," Dan Rather said. "I have a call to make."

The Reporter for the Villages Sun looked him up and down and said, "Courage."

"That's it. Nobody says that to me anymore." He punches the diminutive Oldson in the stomach and takes the phone, dials the number and then waits. "Hey Mom, you wouldn't believe what's happening..."

Oldson finds a bank of phones down the hall but they're all taken. Suddenly a man wearing a big letter S flies down the hall and lands next to the reporter. saying "I've got a bigger story for you."

"So who are you?" asks the non-plussed reporter.

"Well, I'm just Superman, that's all. I've been going around here for thirty years saving people and nobody seems to give a kryptonite cupcake or even really notice. Never connected the dots between all these guys showing up dressed in the same ridiculous flying suit? Never figured it might be the same one, that he might like a little recognition?"

"I guess you should have gotten a new marketing team after about ten years. Right now we've got bigger stuff than you going on, mole people living under the Villages and Perry Mason accusing Jesus of rape and the judge has three teats. You better get in line while you can, Buster. It keeps getting longer."

"Why you ungrateful whelp. Do you know how many times I've pulled your fat out of the fire? And that ditzy broad Lois Plain?"

"Now that you mention it, we did have some close calls that were hard to explain."

Superman folded his arms across his chest. "Exactly."

"Well, look. I gotta go. Why don't you come around to the Sun some time and we'll talk more about it. Right now I have to find a phone.booth."

"Welcome to my world."

"Yeah. See ya."

But not Jesus, the Man of Steel mused as Jimmy Oldson shrank in the distance. He thinks he's just going to show up after two thousand years and pick up where he left off? We'll see about that.

"Pete, this is perfect," Ed Asner said with gusto. "In a little while I'm going over to that trial and state that irrefutably there is a civilization going on under The Villages, probably been there thousands of years. That hits the news we'll just sit back and take orders for sonograms."

"Oh sure. But how you gonna convince anybody from those pictures?"

"Pete, you're such an infant. I'm the expert. People believe experts. They organize their lives around experts. And we did register something down there. I'll just take that and run with it. And if you don't want to get sucked down like Joe Beasley and come back as a colored guy, you better check out your own yard."

"Sure. And then we sell them a steel subfloor that they can't get sucked through."

Asner slapped Pete on the back. "Now you're talkin' Pete. That's the stuff. People love to buy insurance. They'll complain about income tax but they pay off the mortgage and keep right on paying thousands of dollars against the one in a million chance their house burns down. And if it does burn down, good chance they'll go up with it."

"What we got here is a clear and present danger."

"We can't miss."

"But how do we know the floor's gonna work?"

"Because we're experts."

Agzorf and Gleeep have just invented the *Personal Surface Sucker* so every household can have one and people can suck down a fatone whenever they need to, and the inventors don't have to worry about fulfillment.

"How will they know how to aim it at the fatones we made?"

Gleeep looked a little fraught. "*I* haven't even figured out how to do that. I don't know if it's possible. Anyway, they're mostly all fat. Our customers can just set the dial at 75% fat content. They can't go wrong. And we can put our machine under the school they built for all the little fatones. You know, talking about this is making me hungry."

The doors flew open and Ed Asner came barreling into the Sumter County Courtroom.

Perry Mason stood. "I call as my next witness Ed Asner, President of Seismology R Us."

Cheeselton Burger sprang up. "Ed Asner is an actor. Since when is he a geology expert?"

Asner presented to Perry Mason his documentation and Mason handed it to Judge Violet.. "Everything looks in order," says Violet. "I actually thought Ed Asner was dead."

"Like Joe Beasley?" Burger quipped.

"That will be enough of that," Judge Violet admonished.

"Meaning no unjustified disrespect to the court," Burger said, "that wouldn't be a problem. Hell, he probably is dead. So what? It would be a violation of his civil rights to keep him from testifying."

Pontius Violet slammed her gavel. "That will be e*nuff,* Mr. Burger. Another such outburst and I'll hold you in contempt of ort."

"Contempt of what?"

"Contempt of ort."

"Judge, are you al..."

"Just carry on Mr. Burger. Or I'll find you in something."

"Yes, ma'am."

Asner took his place in the witness stand, raised his right hand and with a FWOOP promptly disappeared.

"Gleeep look! I got one."

"And nice and fat, too. See? They don't have to all be the same."

"So we're not throwing this one back?"

"No way. Call the neighbors."

Few spectators actually were looking at the seismologist when he ceased to be there. The few who were looking at him failed to comprehend what they had suddenly not seen, disappearance being too far from their usual experience. People do appearance much better. The result was a brief search for him followed by skepticism that he ever had been there.

"Mr. Mason apparently summoned a hologram to testify and it became unplugged. If he can bring it back, I promise not to challenge its authenticity."

"I thank Cheeselton for the magnanimity of his gesture, however it was meant to demean the witness. I assure the court that Mr. Asner was no hologram and his disappearance testifies more eloquently than any papers he would have interpreted."

On furlough from Heaven to exonerate Joe Beasley while establishing that Beasley was not the second coming, zombie Christ walked in and introduced himself, then started to make his case before Pontius Violet.

Jesus approached the bench. "First off," he said, "I can't believe your name is Pontius Violet. It's like Someone, I wonder Who, is just messing with me."

"Paul," Perry Mason said, "Keep tabs on that man, put him up in a motel if you can. I want to talk to him."

"You got it. Do you think he could be who he says he is?"

Mason looked his investigator square in the eye. "At this point," he said gravely, "it's even money."

"Bailiff, get this guy out of here before I crucify him or something."

"No. Wait. I can prove I'm the son of God. I can do tricks. Who's got some water?"

Just then Superman busted through a side wall of the courtroom, killing Emily Barnhorst with a flying cinder block.

"Shit," Superman said, "I sure hope she had it coming," and he turned around and launched back out to where he'd come from.

170

"Your honor," the prosecutor whined, "Superman just killed one of the witnesses. I don't even know why he's here. I don't know what's going to happen next. Can we have a recess?"

"Why not? Court is adjourned. We'll have a fresh start tomorrow."

23

J immy Oldson wrapped fifty percent of his arms around his woman. "Maxine, please just sit here with me and don't turn into an aardvark or something."

"Okay."

"Maxine, my love, it's like I'm frozen. I don't know what to report first.

"Well, maybe you should report something last and work your way to the first."

"That's a good idea. I'll probably try that. But the thing is ... I don't even know what's news anymore. It's like there's nothing normal to compare anything with."

"My poor man. Always grappling with the world, trying to understand everything so you can protect your family from it."

"That's right. It used to be just my Mom. Now it's my woman and my weird-ass child that looks like Donald Trump. I couldn't even give you a normal baby. It's like you're in an avalanche, with rocks coming down all around ...and going sideways too. And I don't know whether to try to catch all the rocks or pull you out but it's too big to reach the other side."

"I don't even think that S Man could do it." Tears streaked Maxine's face. "But I think you'll do it, my man. I have faith in you and our love. What if we go away from here? Maybe it's just The Villages influence. We could get your Mom and move to Kansas."

"That just might work. Things must be normal there."

"Well they do have tornadoes. What if the tornadoes start going crazy?"

"I don't think they will, my love. But just to be on the safe side, we could try Orla Vista, move in with Mom for awhile."

"She hasn't exactly bonded with the baby you know. Or me."

"That's true. Her house does remind me of that priest's room in The Omen, where he had all those crucifixes everywhere."

"Well, you know, I've never been there. That's just since the baby, isn't it?

"Never went to church in her life. Now she doesn't miss a service, sometimes just goes there and sits by herself. Orla Vista Baptist Church, sits on the step if it's closed."

"I guess we're back to Kansas."

"Yeah but I can't just leave Mr. White here running the paper without me."

"Kansas is pretty far. It could be just a Florida thing. You could send us to Georgia until sanity returns."

"But how can I save you if you're in Georgia?"

"Sending us to Georgia might be saving us."

"Golly. You're right. I'd miss you so much but I could visit," Jimmy said with energy, finally seeing a clear course of action. "I'll find you a place on the internet. And maybe Mom too."

"Yes. Maybe."

Just then the baby started screaming the clearly articulated "Tits!"

The trial finally resumed and was rushed to conclusion at the request of the FBI. In his closing remarks, Cheeselton Burger said, "Ladies and gentlemen of the jury, two can play at this game. I submit to you, based on the testimony of Judge Violet, you must find the defendant guilty on both charges because if that did happen to be Beasley inside that black skin, then the black guy must have killed and eaten Joe Beasley to get him in there. And if it wasn't Joe in there then he still must have done it because he was the only unemployed black guy around. Keep the world safe. It's in your hands."

Under the direction of Pontius Violet, Jesus' black body was found guilty regardless of who was inside and sentenced to a visit with Old Sparky for the attempted rape of Maxine Falderall and the brutal murder of Joe Beasley. This would leave Jesus with nothing to change back into but a charred body as bad as the one he had now– in other words the rest of eternity as a zombie, ruining Woodstock for him. Such can be the price of vanity.

Joe Beasley had with surprising speed gone from King of the Villages to his soul in Jesus' body rotting in the Death House at Starke for his own murder.

After a lot of crying Joe was trying to be philosophical about it. "Well, killing yourself is illegal, I think, so this is the first chance they had to prosecute somebody for it. Can't blame 'em for getting excited about it, probably keep their voters happy. Seems like Jesus' body attracts executions. I wonder why. Anyhow, this damn... darn sure should get me into Heaven. It was a good run down here but guess I'll start looking to the long run. I hope they give me a new dick up there."

"How do I get myself into these fixes?" Jesus berated himself, eternally unraveling head in forever crumbling hands.

With Perry Mason's first defeat, the fabric of society began unraveling as well.

24

Disguised as Mary Poppins, Vladamir Putin had visited Donald Trump in the Mara Logo secret bathroom of joy and offered a screwdriver to the proprietor who had no more experience with the drink then the tool, never having tasted alcohol. In a sexo-political baldo midget and orange fat guy frenzy he drank it and instantly became an alcoholic, validating his lifelong abstinence. Perhaps he should have started with near-beer.

Nevertheless, as the open landscape warms in the rising sun of The Villages, remnants of the night's coolness linger under shrubbery. A few blocks north of Lake Humpter, former United States President Donald Trump hugs himself in a litter of empty Sterno cans. We find him shivering beneath the protective canopy of the most habitable stand of azaleas in Lake Humpter Square, repeating over and over "Just Grab it by the pussy." and occasionally wondering why. "I wish those damn ducks would get here," he says to himself through chattering teeth. "They're probably looking for that old bitch with the rum cake."

President Trump heard a light shuffling outside the flower bed and his spirits soared. The bumpy bill of a muscovy duck poked through the foliage followed by two other muscovies and a coot. "About time you got here," Trump emoted, sitting up. "I've been saving this." Still wearing the orange suit from the day he began the Sabbatical from his station in life, the orange haired freedom fighter hoisted a can of Sterno to his comrades. The middle duck lifted its tail feathers and squirted in appreciation. Outside the azaleas Secret Service agents roasted wienies.

Orange was Trump's color, like it had contaminated him from the hair down; promoting a benign, citrus-like visage when he wasn't speaking. "Alright you stupid ducks," he toasted. "Remeat after pee. What can be done can be undone. What has been spoiled can be despoiled. Burrrrap!"

The ducks became restless. Ever a calm head, the coot glanced sharply at them with a look that said, Give him a chance. He might still have connections.

Donald Trump continued," As you know, we have been experimenting with the rubber duck head I invented, with the help of my people, many people, really great Americans, not Mexicans or Canadians or Marzipans, with greatest, greater in the world, successfulness. Really tip top...I didn't need the help but... there you go, help happens. What can you do? Just go in it, that's all, greatly. No Little Don Junior so disguised has been captured and shipped off." Two of the ducks opened their bills wide, as if yawning. "We must work on getting them to stay on

177

better." One duck began preening while the other two faced the former president with blank expressions, one of them scaring himself as he habitually did, by contemplating that he used to be the liquid inside an egg. "Oh, hell. You're just a bunch of damn ducks. You can't even vote. Well maybe you can. I don't know. Nobody knows. Can anybody find out?"

"Yeah, ducks can vote," yells a secret service man.

Another agent swats him. "Hey Clint. We're not supposed to interfere. You know, the Star Trek policy of non-intervention. No telling what could happen on Planet Trump because of what you just said."

"Yeah, yeah. Alright. I couldn't resist."

"Screw this blather, Mr. President! Let's go out and desecrate something, Goofy boomed from above the bush tops. Trump looked up but saw mainly the underside of azalea leaves and light blue flowers. Don't stand there talking to me, you stupid idiot. Get in here."

"Can't do it, boss. You're too ducked up."

With that he pushed the coot's tolerance and the coot led the muscovies back to their uncertain fate on the softshell turtle infested water, grotesque bills pointed upward with disdain as they crossed the lake-shore sidewalk. After Clint frisked him, Goofy stepped to the middle of the azaleas and plopped down, snapping a branch.

"You broke one of my roof rafters, you goofy sonofabitch. Did you at least bring a drinking vessel? And

178

next time, crawl in, will you?"

"Uh-hilt! Goofy blurted his cartoon counterpart's trade. mark sound. "Don't mind if I do. I got a storyfoam cup outta the rubbish bin."

"Dammit. You know styrofoam won't hold this stuff."

"Gotcha, didn't I? Here. Fill my Coke can." The giant rubber head cocked inquisitively. "Revolution's off again, eh, Prez? Here's to happier days." Goofy sniffed the cooking fuel before substituting a vodka pint at his enormous lips.

"This revolution can never take a nap," Trump declared in the manner of John Brown the Cuban Exile halibut from Venus. Swiveling to face his suitcase, he popped it open gravely. Let's take a stroll as soon as I'm changed.

"Meet you outside," Goofy said, averting his gaze from an unadorned ex-president to the guano enriched Lake Humpter with its wrinkled motor oil algae and styrofoam cup islands.

"Listen, Goofy," the altered Trump said half an hour later, squatting with white skirt crumpled around him like the last sugarplum fairy dying on the sidewalk of global warming. But it was just the middle of Lake Humpter Square encircled by Secret Service agents blocking the view with a curtain. "The problem with the world today is nobody exhibits their feces. Hell. You remember the first few times you put a poopy in the potty? Your parents thought that was wonderful. Just the best, best thing that ever was or ever could be produced by anybody, as good as

179

anybody could make, maybe better. You thought you could probably make a living at it. Looked like they were going to put it in a glass case and set it on a prominent place, maybe a hutch, because you did such a good job, just right. Yeah, a hutch. Somewhere. In somebody's house. But not our house, no, maybe not that good. Maybe they sold it already. Then one day, Mommy says, 'Come on, Donald. From now on those go in the toilet where we can flush them away because we don't want to see them anymore.' So you spend the rest of your life trying to make your parents proud again but what you'd really like to do is just show them your shit and get on with life."

Trump shifted his feet slightly, precariously maintaining balance holding Goofy's hand, and grimaced for ten seconds, carefully laying the foundation.

"Look at all these dogs. Why are they so happy? Because a dog doesn't just take a dump. He presents his product to the world. He's not taught to be ashamed and flush away the main result of his existence. A dog picks a high traffic area where his monument will be seen, sniffed, judged, eaten and possibly even nominated by his peers. But no, that's not enough for me. I have to be President of the United States and my parents still don't give a frog's anus. And everybody else makes fun of me. Not nice, no, no, not very nice. Not even greatly polite. My dad was King of the KKK. It's hard to shit that big."

"Your day to be Snow White?" Goofy tried to change the subject.

Trump became quiet as his face assumed the blank gaze of sublime concentration most often seen on defecating Irish setters. He spread the second layer, then rose slowly, adjusting his apron and smoothing it down.

"No, I just Just felt like it," he said, admiring the deposit as he wiggled into his giant underpants. "How'd you know it was me? It was my calling card, wasn't it? Get back here, Goof. Being half dog and half man, you're caught right in the middle of this. Dogs wouldn't even think about wiping. And why do you suppose that is? Why?" Snow White jabbed Goofy in the chest. "Because what's the good of displaying the stuff if nobody knows it's yours??!"

Goofy took a long hit from the bottle.

"Of course my shit's bigger and better than anyone else's so you know people would just say, 'Hey look. There's Donald Trump's shit. Nobody else could have done that. Right there, made America great again.

"Pay attention, you goddamn homeless drain on society. Dogs are always trying to name the artist. Fido sniffs Rex and says, 'Say, I saw that magnificent pile you planted over on 14th Street. Nice colors. Good one. Or. Wow! I didn't see that one, Bob. Where is it?'"

"How are people gonna know this is yours, Donald? Looks the same to me as any other shit, maybe a little nastier."

"Never call me that," Trump says, sitting on Goofy's head.

"Okay, okay. Just don't sit on my head anymore. Uh-hilt."

"Mirror mirror on the wall, who has the best, the really

best turds of all?"

"U-hilt. You do Mr. President."

"Alright, I'll get off your head. Just remember what I said. Now let's get outta here and find Benedict Arnold Pence."

The nipples of the mother- fathers of the Don Trump Jr. clones secreted an oily corruption resembling cappuccino and cigaret butts, savored by the offspring; but the owners of the nipples had lost interest pretty quickly in motherhood, especially the nursing part, fearing their enjoyment of that duty made them gay. The ones who were gay just took it in stride. Either way most of the Trump Jr. clones went feral and The Villages Public Works Department initiated a program to catch and paint little suits on them, then turn them loose again to roam The Villages like ponderous squirrels, surviving on whatever nutrition people would toss to them. The president -in-exile was a big proponent of this as he planned to buy The Villages and change the name to Trump World. Every time Trump showed up at city hall with a bag full, the clerk naturally assumed it was just some MAGA fat guy in a Trump costume, like all the Mike Pence look-alikes running around.

"That sissy Pence," Trump twitted, "he can't stop me now. Because I'm stopping him." Anyway, good way to avoid all those boring problems, he mused. What a great disguise. They'd never let the world know I'm living in the bushes...these great bushes, very great... maybe I'll make bushes great again...but not george bushes, no... not that

182

kind that never were great…or kind, just this great kind, greatest great best.

25

Mike Pence considers the Don juniors an abomination and a poke in the eye of God, who told him once that he likes to make people one at a time, three absolute tops, and usually subtly different, (and surely not born of the gastrointestinal tract). He was covertly trapping the toddlers and shipping them to a duck and elephant-hunting ranch in Ohio where adult Don Junior received them.

In accordance with God's directives toward capitalism, Pence did sell some into slavery to the Saudis. Barney Jenkins encountered him one day dropping one into a bag.

"Hey," Jenkins accosted him, "you're that guy that isn't Mike Pence, right? Or are you the one who is. You look so much the same you know."

"No, I told you, I'm not Mike Pence. Mike Pence is in Washington D.C., like many other people. Some look like Mike Pence and some don't."

"Okay, you're not Mike Pence. Can I call you Kemosabi? Because you look like one. That way I can remember it."

Pence brightened. Yes, I do look like a kemosabi, he thought.

"It's easier to remember your name that way. It means sheep anus."

Stay calm, Pence told himself. You were the vice president of the United States once, one bullet away from The Job. This creep doesn't matter. Keep looking at the big picture. "Yeah, sure, that's smart."

"So what are you doing with that baby? Why you bagging it? This ain't Publix."

"If you must know, I work for The Villages. We're rounding these things up for a display."

"I'm no big baby's rights fanatic but you're handling them pretty rough."

"Well, Mr. John Q. Public, I wouldn't worry about it. You've seen the bag the stork carries them in, right? It's the same thing. Babies like being all jumbled up. Reminds them of the good old days before they were born or before they were aborted, however you want to look at it."

"Where's your uniform?"

"I'm an executive. I don't wear one."

"I don't believe you. I'm callin' the cops."

God, I hate living in the cell phone age, Pence thinks.

"Alright, look. I am Mike Pence. Alright?!? Recent vice president of the United States. Should still be vice president. So I can do whatever the Hell I want. And right now I'm on a mission."

Two of Trump's secret service men have been behind a

hedge eavesdropping on the conversation. "Alright," Morey whispers, "it *is* him."

"Now wadda we do?"

"I guess we should notify his secret service team."

Suddenly Donald Trump appears with the rest of his agents. "That's alright guys. Back off. I've got this."

"Waddaya got there, Pencey? Or should I say Little Worm Boy?"

"Oh, hello Mr. President. Nothing to see here."

"I'll say it again," Trump said, shifting feet and cocking his head sideways. "You putting my family in that sack? Because if you are, I don't like that. It's not very great. Not very great at all. But that's right because you're not very great. We found that out, didn't we, Wormo the Not Great? Everybody, the whole entire country, the whole constellation found out, Mike Pence is not very great; not very great at all.

"Do you think you're great Mike? Do you think you're even anything, you disloyal dog puke I pulled up from nowhere? You pasty faced Q-Tip? I wouldn't do you if you were the last woman on Earth. You know, I was talking to my son. He had something very interesting to tell me. What do you think it was Mike? Do you have any ideas what it might be?"

"You're both Assholes, if you need to know," Barney Jenkins interjected himself. Two agents walked him away.

"Whoever that was, he was right half the time," Trump said. "That's a better rate than anybody else I can think of. Get his name. That's my new chief of staff."

Jenkins tried to yell something over his shoulder but it was muffled. The Secret Service confiscated the sack.

Aggravated by all these miniatures of himself competing for his father's love, Don Junior turned them loose on receipt from Mike Pence. He shut his eyes and counted off thirty seconds, then yelled, "Ready or not, here I come."

"Just to be sporting," he thought, "I'll hunt them with my eyes shut. I'll listen for gurgling and crying and rustling in the leaves, things like that. Maybe farting too. That would be a clue."

So he hunted them down that way and on locating one, he would in the direction of the telltale sound separate its molecules with a 12 gauge shotgun, selling the remains as magic fertilizer to nearby farmers. He had one sushied and in case it would give him super powers, he ate one alive. Of course he already had caged a half dozen in a secret corner of the ranch against the day his organs start to fail.

Vilageers and sometimes visitors began disappearing randomly, leaving no trace. Occasionally a spouse would be snatched walking hand in hand with its mate. In this Jimmy the Geek found a new game. Due to the randomness of the disappearances, the odds were pretty even across the board although there were long shots like the Smiths who had purchased from Seismology R Us a lead lined steel floor. Though the Geek did not believe in the subterranean population, each disappearance was labeled a premature burial, just to cash in on the growing urban myth. Agzorf and Gleeep having perfected the technology, nobody got taken half-away anymore, or returned.

"Maxine, you know this rumor about people getting snatched underground?"

"Of course, Jimmy. It happened to you."

"Sometimes I don't even believe that anymore. It feels more like a dream."

"Then what do you think is happening to these other people?"

"I have a hunch and what a story it would be,"

"Tell me, star reporter. What is it?"

Oldson turned and held Maxine by the shoulders. "What if soylent green is people? What if this is a woke thing that's going to spread across the planet to solve world hunger?"

"How could that work?"

"Don't you see Maxine? Feeding people with people. It's killing two birds with one idea. They're cutting down the population while feeding the remainder with a product that costs nothing to produce."

"What, Jimmy?"

"People, Maxine. People. And they can blame it on these made-up, hipster subterranean people eaters."

"Maxine. Maxine. Where did you go? Nooo! Noooo!"

The star reporter for a great metropolitan newspaper, with his money from the National Enquirer, bought a backhoe. He purchased the graphs from Seismology R Us and could be seen at any time on any piece of not yet built-on earth, digging. Some nights he slept, armed with a pistol, on the bench where he had been abducted so long ago. Verry White often checked on him, bringing hot cocoa or adjusting his blanket in a fatherly manner. A couple times Oldson espied the Donald Trump look-alike with his pretend secret service crew but he was no longer interested in any other stories. After two months, during which his toddler just kind of wandered off in disgust, Jimmy had run out of land and quit. But he never gave up, whenever he walked through The Villages calling her name through a bullhorn and putting stethoscope to ground.

The *Car 54 where are You?* Club members normally drove around in their golfcarts hollering the name of their club. Another member hearing this would call out, "Over here." Then the chase was on, the pursuer or pursuers calling out the question and the pursued required to always respond "over here" until caught. Sympathetic to Oldson's cause they substituted Maxine in their game but they never again got an answer. Eventually the club split into two factions – the original and the Maxiners, which dichotomy was frustrating and led to the dissolution of the club. It was a sad thing for all concerned.

It's high noon in The Villages

As Gary Cooper hopped on Old Thunder and galloped out of town, Mike Pense and Donald Trump, each reinforced by his own Secret Service squad faced off across fifty feet of space on the neutral podiums of Spanish Bedsprings. At least one hundred feet distance was required of spectators. Winning the coin toss, Trump made Pence go first. His agents could be heard murmuring, "Rumble, rumble."

Pence relished the catharthis: "You ruined my life, you hulking tub of talking lard blubber. 'Come on Mike. Be my running mate. I need an albino on the ticket for the white supremacists. I have a little too much color. We'll be a team,' you said. 'This is the train to the top of the world and I'm reaching out my grubby little hand to you. Grab it now and ride with me or just stand there and spend the rest of your mediocre life wondering what went wrong.' That's what you said. Well, I sure don't have to wonder what went wrong, you were right about that, because I know exactly what that was. You're Mr. Global. You ran for president of the United States as a business venture. So there I am, from Governor of Indiana to Vice President of Trump Enterprises. There's a fun ride."

"So I ruined your life. How could I ruin something that crummy? What did you have? Safeness? A reputation for sanity? You didn't even have a reputation. Nobody in the whole constellation ever heard of you. You were the Cassius Clay of the moon. Just as famous there as he was. You were great at one thing – at being nothing. You were the most zero has ever been, I'll give you that – probably the biggest zero in history. My mistake Mike, I admit it. Well, maybe not an actual mistake. Let's say I wildly overestimated your potential. I'm just too good, too yummy, if I have a fault. I always see the best in people, what I think they can become, not what they're wasting their time being. Guess I went overboard in your case. You should have come with a warning label, Pence: **what you see is what you get**. And not a damn thing more."

"Yeah? I'll admit that slogan wouldn't fit you. There's a whole lot more to you than meets the eye, isn't there? And that's saying something because a whole lot of you meets the eye, you stranded blue whale with your soft little high pitched voice. I recall you saying you were running for President, you didn't have a brain cell's chance in Washington of winning but it was sure to be a hell of a ride. The only chance I'd ever have of breaking out, of putting God back in the White House. Had the greatest slogan in history, it didn't mean a thing but Hilary was so bad, it just might work. And afterwards your whole life will be elevated, to the rare level of people who ran for president because, you know Mike, I don't make it full term, you're the President of the United States. How's them apples? you asked me. You didn't mention that if that didn't work, you were fully capable of inviting an armed mob to invade the capitol. Did you? And then put me in the wholly untenable spot of having to either disobey my president, or betray my constitution, which I had previously suspected of being on the same team. I don't see a good side to that for me. Do you, you overinflated goat stomach?"

"Beached whale? Goat stomach? Is that all you got after I #@%&#! you over like I did? I want to say you remind me of cat puke but I don't want to insult cat ..."

191

"Alright, Agzorf, are you ready?"

"I'm ready Gleeep. Are you ready?"

"Ready. Alright, on the count of three, two at once.

"One, two...

Of course there were Donald Trump sightings all over the midwest for awhile, more than Bigfoot at first and Mike Pence sightings mostly in Jellystone National Park and, oddly, Papua New Guinea. So many that it became a federal crime to impersonate either one of them due to the strain on the Secret Service.

Since neither Pence nor Trump was occupying public office at the time of their unorthodox exit together, very little investigating was done, pretty much filed under Shit that Happens. Time to move on.

Some in the CIA thought it should be attributed to space aliens, fitting nicely with the government's recent decision to acknowledge their existence and scare people into funding the Space Farce; but Jeb Bush was in charge of that department and he lacked the energy.

There was a rumor that, digging in someone's yard, Jimmy Oldson found a MAGA cap but nobody cared enough to look into it.

Three months later Pontius Violet sold her life story to Titsosterone Magazine and retired from the bench. God and Jesus were back in their heaven and God promised Jesus a new body for Woodstock.

"For God's sake just don't get this one crucified," God said.

Jesus said, "Thanks Dad, I won't" and tickled him in the arm pit. Then God picked him up and they looked deeply into each others' eyeballs and bonded.

And that, children, is the story of how Jesus and God became One. It all happened in The Villages.